Garth BROOKS

STERLING
New York

An Imprint of Sterling Publishing
1166 Avenue of the Americas
New York, NY 10036

STERLING and the distinctive Sterling logo are registered trademarks of Sterling Publishing Co., Inc.

© 2015 by Essential Works Limited

Production by Essential Works

ISBN 978-1-4549-1743-4

Distributed in Canada by Sterling Publishing
c/o Canadian Manda Group, 664 Annette Street
Toronto, Ontario, Canada M6S 2C8

Distributed in the United Kingdom by GMC Distribution Services
Castle Place, 166 High Street, Lewes, East Sussex, England BN7 1XU

Distributed in Australia by Capricorn Link (Australia) Pty. Ltd.
P.O. Box 704, Windsor, NSW 2756, Australia

For information about custom editions, special sales, and premium and corporate purchases, please contact
Sterling Special Sales at 800-805-5489 or specialsales@sterlingpublishing.com.

Manufactured in China

2 4 6 8 10 9 7 5 3 1

www.sterlingpublishing.com

Garth BROOKS

THE ILLUSTRATED STORY

ANDREW VAUGHAN

STERLING
New York

CONTENTS

INTRODUCTION

mazingly, this is the first fully illustrated book to tell the remarkable story of one of the biggest-selling solo artists in the world. Exactly why it's the first such book on the world's most famous singing cowboy, a graduate of media and advertising studies, the man who did so much in the 1990s to change the visual, aural, and cultural landscape of country music—and in the process changing the physical shape of the city of Nashville—strikes me as odd. Throughout his career—and even before he was famous—Garth was always self-deprecating about his looks, his weight, and his hairline, but the fact is that he became a publicly adored star of stage and screen. How his music was presented visually was always of prime importance to Garth, and how he dressed for public appearances was also of high importance.

Garth broke through at a time when male country music stars were generally conservative, wore big hats and fancy boots, and strummed acoustic guitars, so that was what he did. Or, rather, kind of did. After making a couple of records and videos in which he looked like George Strait, Alan Jackson, or Clint Black did in their music videos, Garth happened upon a distinct, if not distinctly different, look and began to wear brightly colored, big-patterned rodeo shirts that visually marked him apart from his fellow musicians on stage and on the CD racks. It was a small but distinctive move by a man who would, over the course of the decade, change the look, sound, and impact of country music completely.

When Garth Brooks jumped on stage to perform at President Obama's inauguration in Washington, DC, in 2009, it was an official recognition that the singing cowboy from Oklahoma had forged himself a unique position in pop music history. That performance marked twenty years at the top for the best-selling solo artist in the history of recorded music, but came at a time when he was not even supposed to be in the public spotlight. Garth's career has been astoundingly eventful.

As one of the first writers to interview Garth Brooks, I have followed his career closely, interviewed him regularly in the United States and overseas, and watched him rise to the top, unravel, withdraw, and then come back to the top. I first met Garth Brooks at a small, smoky club in Nashville called the Cockeyed Camel in 1988. The singer was raw and nervous, and performed solo to a handful of barely interested diners and drinkers. There was nothing to suggest that this was a superstar in the making, but still, he was introduced to me by a publicity agent whose opinion I valued as being "the future of country music," and I'd never heard this PR enthuse so about a newcomer before.

RIGHT: Garth Brooks–the most successful male singing star of any genre.

ABOVE: Garth demonstrating some of the rock concert elements that he included in his shows, as he swings above the crowd.

I didn't realize it at the time, but Garth's interview with me in that dive bar was the first interaction he'd had with the international press. It was also the first of many interviews between us—indeed I may well have interviewed Garth Brooks more times than any other journalist.

Back then I was in Nashville to interview a handful of young acts for my first book, *Who's Who in New Country*, and as my own country music writing and PR career grew and developed, so our paths crossed in numerous ways. Garth, his wife Sandy, and I would regularly have breakfast—the pair of them used to babysit for my girlfriend of the time. Brooks was making his way, making friends and contacts, as was I. We both knew the same people, ran in the same circles, and I watched,

"No matter what you say you might do, you never really know until you're in the moment. Every situation is so different."

GARTH BROOKS

fascinated by his incredible rise to superstardom from the ground up. At a time when Nashville was looking outward to an international market, I was lucky enough to have special access at events and functions, courtesy of being at the time a UK-based writer. When I was asked to launch the UK's first glossy monthly country music magazine in 1993, it was funded primarily thanks to Brooks's mass global popularity. A Garth Brooks photo on the cover of the magazine sold three times the number of copies that any other artist managed. Since Brooks was determined to take on the world, our professional relationship blossomed as he toured internationally in the mid-1990s. For a long time Garth's website carried a quote from my magazine, *Country Music International,* on its home page.

During our face-to-face chats Brooks's special talent became obvious. He drew his interviewers in, looked directly and intently into their eyes, thought deeply about every question, and acted like a long-lost cousin, so glad to finally touch base and reconnect with his interrogators. Whether genuine or contrived, his interpersonal skills were remarkable and would take him all that way from Oklahoma to the White House. By October 2000 he had become, in the space of the previous decade, the best-selling solo artist in the history of recorded music.

Brooks's integration of rock elements into his recordings and live performances made him so popular that after dominating the country single and country album charts he quickly crossed over into the mainstream pop arena, taking country music to a larger, wider audience than any other artists had managed—including Johnny Cash and Willie Nelson. In the United States alone, his albums sold more than 100 million copies. *Ropin' the Wind*, Brooks's third album, released in September 1991, was the first ever to debut at No. 1 on both the *Billboard* Top 200 Album Chart and the *Billboard* Top Country Albums Chart. *The Chase* (1992) and

In Pieces (1993) were the second and third albums to do so. *Sevens* (1997) and *Double Live* (1998) also accomplished this feat. Brooks's television credits include eight specials for NBC: *This Is Garth Brooks* (first airing January 1992); *This Is Garth Brooks, Too!* (May 1994); *Garth Brooks: The Hits* (January 1995); *Tryin' to Rope the World* (December 1995); *Garth Brooks: Ireland and Back* (March 1998); *Garth Brooks Double Live* (November 1998); *In the Life of Chris Gaines* (September 1999); and *Garth Brooks and the Magic of Christmas* (December 1999).

On August 7, 1997, Brooks drew the largest crowd ever to attend a concert in New York's Central Park. The simultaneous live broadcast, *Garth Live from Central Park*, was the highest-rated original program on HBO that year, as well as the most-watched special on cable television in 1997, drawing 14.6 million television viewers. The special outperformed all the broadcasts during that time slot including "three of the four major networks combined," according to Nielsen ratings.

Over the course of his career, Brooks has received virtually every accolade the recording industry can bestow on an artist. In addition to his Grammys, American Music Awards, Country Music Association awards, Academy of Country Music awards, and People's Choice trophies, he was named artist of the '90s at the 1997 Blockbuster Entertainment Awards and Artist of the Decade by both the American Music Awards in 2000 and the Academy of Country Music in 1999. Brooks's live concerts were equally pace-setting and praised publicly as well as critically.

However, troubled by conflicts he felt between career and family, in 2001 Brooks officially retired from recording and performing. During this time he sold millions of albums through an exclusive distribution deal with Wal-Mart and sporadically released new singles. In 2005, Brooks started a partial comeback, and in 2009, he announced the end of his retirement and that December began a multi-year concert deal with the Encore Hotel and Casino on the Las Vegas Strip. In November 2010, Brooks announced a benefit concert in Nashville for victims of the May floods in Tennessee. The 100,000 tickets were sold in just an hour, and Brooks announced eight more shows. It was the biggest one-day sale in the venue's history.

When he retired in 2001, Garth stated that he would stay off the road (and out of the studio) until his third daughter, Allie, left home to attend college—he was retiring in order to see more of his three kids, and after divorcing Sandy in 2001, the pair agreed to share the responsibility of raising them. It wasn't long before Garth was aided in his home by second wife, international singing star Trisha Yearwood (they married in 2005). As his Vegas residency—enabled by the loan of a jet plane that got the singer from Nevada and back home to Oklahoma every Monday morning—came to an end in 2012, Garth hinted that he'd soon be back performing full time, and in different places, too.

ABOVE: Garth and team celebrate music live on stage, 2015.

FOLLOWING PAGES: Trisha Yearwood and Garth Brooks in tune together.

In 2013, he announced a world tour with Trisha Yearwood. Garth Brooks was back, and as dates were announced through 2014 and 2015 they sold out in record-breaking time.

Garth's career has been a long, strange one (so far), and I'm honored to have borne witness to it. In the following pages (and in full color) I have tried to celebrate his life and music, and to show my appreciation of his rare talent and astounding work.

I hope you enjoy reading it as much as I have writing it.

1

In the Beginning

Garth Brooks made his first public appearance on February 7, 1962, at the St. John Medical Center in Tulsa, Oklahoma. Troyal Garth Brooks (as he was christened) became the final addition to what would now be termed a "blended" family.

Garth was the second child of a second marriage for both his father and mother. Troyal "Raymond" Brooks was an ex-Marine who dabbled on guitar for fun, and Colleen Carroll Brooks had been a moderately successful professional singer in her younger days. She released records as Colleen Carroll and made a few appearances on Red Foley's *Ozark Jubilee* radio and TV show in the 1950s. Raymond and Colleen's first son, Kelly, was a year and a half older than Garth, and both boys had older half-siblings from their parents's previous marriages.

Garth then, was the youngest of six children, and as the baby of the family was usually the center of attention. Clearly much loved, baby Brooks was encouraged in everything that he did.

Garth lived the first few years of his life amid the hustle and bustle of the oil town Tulsa, Oklahoma's second-largest city. In the mid-1960s, and possibly looking for a quieter life, the Brooks family moved about fifteen miles into the country to the small town of Yukon, when Garth was just four years old.

The Brooks home on Yukon Avenue was pure Middle America. Theirs was a modest two-story house befitting a lower-middle-class family, and in keeping with Raymond Brooks's position as a draftsman for the Union of California oil company in Tulsa. According to Garth, life as a kid growing up in Yukon was close to perfect. He told *Playboy*'s Steve Pond in June 1994, "Everything I know about my childhood, everything I feel about my childhood, was nothing but Disneyland. Great place. Growing up in a family that didn't have wealth, a family made up of three families coming together. Mike is from Dad's first marriage, and Jim and Jerry and Betsy are from Mom's first marriage. Then they had Kelly and me. It's three different families coming together, but it worked."

Before Garth Brooks put Yukon on the map it was best known for being situated on the famed Chisolm Trail, so well memorialized in the John Wayne movie of 1948, *Red River*. The town was developed by Czech immigrants as a watering hole for the cowboys driving cattle from Texas to Kansas. There is still a thriving Western and cowboy culture in the area, and tourists regularly visit historic cattle trails, rodeos, and even working ranches.

ABOVE: Garth Brooks's photo from his junior year Yukon High School yearbook, 1979.

PREVIOUS PAGE: An early performance photograph, taken in the late 1980s before Garth began using the radio microphone.

"Oklahoma is a cowboy state," noted Dan Provo, director of the museum in the Oklahoma History Center in Oklahoma City on the Oklahoma tourism site, oktourism.com. "Many people visiting Oklahoma are surprised at the great amount of history relating to cowboys, ranching and cattle trails in Oklahoma." This was a place where Gene Autry's "cowboy code," a very Western take on the medieval, chivalric knight's code, remained alive and well into the twenty-first century. According to the silver screen's singing cowboy: "The cowboy must never shoot first, hit a smaller man, or take unfair advantage. He must never go back on his word or a trust confided in him. He must always tell the truth. He must be gentle with children, the elderly, and animals. He must not advocate or possess racially or religiously intolerant ideas. He must help people in distress. He must be a good worker. He must keep himself clean in thought, speech, action, and personal habits. He must respect women, parents and his nation's laws. The cowboy is a patriot."

> ## "If I have any talent at all it's from God. And mom, who was on Capitol Records."
>
> ### GARTH BROOKS

Garth Brooks may not have been raised around horses, nor never held a branding iron, or roped any steers, but he had an instinctive appreciation of those very American values. It was the John Wayne view of America. As Brooks told *Playboy* in 1994, he had grown up with a genuine affection for the Duke, undoubtedly the most famous cowboy actor of all time. "John Wayne's characters knew what was right and wrong, whether they were the good guy or the bad guy. They might not admit it, but they knew it, and you could see it."

The imagery, values, and mythology of the West would play a significant role in Brooks's music, persona, and image as he rose through the ranks of country music. That record-breaking journey was, most commentators have noted, rooted in two essential character traits:

The first was his ability to think big and reach for goals that were far too lofty and unattainable for most. The second was Brooks's almost superhuman work ethic. Nobody ever worked harder at every aspect of the entertainment business. There's a reason no country artist has ever tried to emulate his autograph-signing session in 1996, at the fairgrounds in Nashville—the sheer effort of will involved in signing his name for fans for twenty-three hours straight is not commonly possessed.

Garth explained to *Rolling Stone*'s Anthony DeCurtis in the April 1, 1993, issue that his parents had very different personalities and that he drew heavily from both. His mother was artistic, a follower of dreams and an eternal optimist. On the other hand, Raymond Brooks, the ex-Marine, was hard working, grounded, down to earth, and lived by the principle of tough love.

"My mom gave me the limitless feeling of dreaming. Mom can be standing on a bridge that is burning like hell and she'll say: 'Well, this bridge'll hold up. I'll just walk right off here.' She had that never-dying hope and faith. My dad worked two jobs, had six kids, and gave them all an opportunity to go to college—he gave me reality."

When the kids were outside the house they were often playing sports, guided by Garth's father, who instilled a deep belief in team ethics among all of them, whether they were throwing hoops in the backyard or playing Little League baseball on teams coached by Mr. Brooks. "I always loved sports," a young and unassuming and still pretty much unknown Garth Brooks told me across a nightclub table in the fall of 1988. "Music kind of took over because I felt I reached my limit as an athlete, but growing up it was a genuine passion and something that taught me the value of practice, hard work, and learning from others."

His major childhood hero was not an actor or singer. It was Pittsburgh Pirates baseball star Roberto Clemente, who excelled in his sport by leading his team to a World Series win in 1971, but also transcended it. Clemente became a national hero after he died when a plane taking supplies to earthquake survivors in Nicaragua crashed on New Year's Eve, 1972.

As Brooks grew up, music filled the rooms at the family home—his dad loved old-time country music, especially George Jones, Johnny Horton, and Merle Haggard. The Brooks family would often sit and listen to the Grand Ole Opry on WSM radio, direct from Nashville, Tennessee.

Garth's mother, Colleen, was more than just a decent singer herself; before her marriage she'd been a successful professional. She put out a single on a Kansas-based label called Cardinal (although Garth has said it was Capitol), and the self-penned

LEFT: Garth in his sophomore year at Yukon High School 1978.

ABOVE: Garth's first place of employment, the Dupree Sports store in Stillwater, Oklahoma.

"No Tellin'" b/w "Blue Bonnet Waltz" (1955) earned good reviews locally and on *Billboard*'s country music pages. "I had what they used to call a cigarette-alto," Colleen explained to the *Oklahoman*'s Barbara Palmer in 1992. "They said I was kind of a cross between Jo Stafford and Frank Sinatra." After three further singles for other independent labels without having a hit, Colleen quit singing professionally in order to raise her family. She was well aware that there was no way for a woman with children, at that time, to do both.

Since Raymond enjoyed playing guitar and Colleen loved to sing, they held what they called "Country Music and Performance Nights" at their house in Yukon most Friday and Saturday nights, when Brooks was young. The family gathered as his father, brother Jerry, and sister Betsy played guitar. Other brother Jim played harmonica, Colleen sang, and the little kids, Kelly and Garth, joined in as best they could, humming through wax paper and combs.

Performance was in his blood then, and it wasn't only music that he was encouraged to take part in playing as a kid, either. Some viewers may have been surprised at Garth's comedic talents when he first hosted that American comedy staple, *Saturday Night Live,* in 1992. After making a witty opening monologue, Brooks performed in full psychedelic gear with fictional '60s band the Electric Gumdrop Convention.

Those acting skills were developed and honed during raucous family nights in Yukon, at which he was usually the star. "I'm always surprised no one says he's funny," his mother told Barbara Palmer of *Oklahoma Today* in 1992. "His first complete sentence was, 'I'm the boss around here.' He kept us all in stitches."

JOHN WAYNE

Like any boy growing up in the 1960s and '70s, Garth Brooks was a fan of cowboy pictures. Television schedules were packed with Western-themed shows that drew viewers to them in the millions—including *Wagon Train* (1957–65), *Bonanza* (1959–73), *Rawhide* (1959–66), *The Virginian* (1962–71), and *High Chaparral* (1967–71).

When not screening their own Western shows, television channels would fill hours of airtime with Western movies made between 1930 (after the invention of talking pictures) and the end of the 1950s. A dominant figure in every Western show and movie was the male hero who stood alone, a fast-drawing, sharp-shooting, law-abiding tough guy who knew what was right and who was wrong. That hero, no matter how troubled and troubling he might have seemed to the impressionable young male viewer, and despite facing the seemingly impossible odds stacked against him, would always fight his way to victory. He would always triumph over the bad guys.

The physical embodiment of the screen Western hero had been set in 1939, in a movie called *Stagecoach*, directed by John Ford and starring John Wayne. Although a veteran of dozens of two-reel Western B-movies by the time he made *Stagecoach*, it took Ford's unique viewfinder to properly turn Wayne's magnificent profile into cinematic legend. With the outbreak of the Second World War, Wayne was cast in the role of contemporary military characters—he was a dashing young naval officer in *Seven Sinners* (1940) with Marlene Dietrich, a downed air force pilot in *Reunion in France* (1942) with Joan Crawford, and a construction engineer building airstrips for the U.S. Navy in the Pacific in *The Fighting Seabees* (1944) with Susan Hayward.

Wayne's on-screen persona rarely altered from the gruff, tough man with a mission. Whether wearing the uniform of the Seventh Cavalry in *She Wore a Yellow Ribbon* (1949), a sheriff's badge in *Rio Bravo* (1959), or a Seattle police lieutenant's raincoat in *McQ* (1974), Wayne exuded authority, power, and an essential American-ness that few of his contemporaries had worn with so much pride and persistence.

Born Marion Robert Morrison in Iowa in 1907, his family moved to Los Angeles in 1916. After failing to get into the U.S. Navy, he won a sports scholarship to play football and study law at the University of South California. That lapsed due to a fractured collarbone (done while surfing), however, and, unable to pay his tuition fees, he left the university. Wayne, who'd worked as a prop boy and extra for John Ford on Tom Mix movies while a student, decided to go into the movie business full time and became an extra and bit-part player in silent Westerns.

Wayne's nickname, the Duke, was given to him when he was a small boy, by a local fireman (according to legend) who named him Little Duke because he regularly walked an Airedale named Duke who was almost as big as the young boy. Not being fond of his given name, Wayne asked everyone to call him Duke, even after he'd become world famous as John Wayne. He took the Wayne professional name in 1930, after it was suggested to him by the director Raoul Walsh, who cast him as a lead character in Hollywood's first externally shot, big-budget talking Western, *The Big Trail*. Unfortunately, the movie, shot in 70mm widescreen format, couldn't be shown in many theaters and it bombed (having cost more than $2 million to make). For the next decade Wayne played supporting roles in A-list movies and second lead in more than 80

THE DUKE

"horse opera" Westerns, as he called them. But with *Stagecoach* his career took off. Wayne's role as the initially unlikeable Marine sergeant in *The Sands of Iwo Jima* (1949) cemented his position as America's prime self-sacrificing screen hero. His death at the movie's end and subsequent touching revelation via a letter written to his son left many viewers in tears. Throughout the movie Wayne and his troop, who represent America's endeavors in World War II, are presented as great symbols of valor and Christian value.

Wayne's staunch support for Republican values and glorification of his country's armed forces on screen (he never served in any capacity) made him an enemy of the supporters of the 1960s-era counterculture; he produced, directed, and starred in the only movie to actively support America's war in Vietnam, *The Green Berets* (1968). Shot at Fort Benning, Georgia, the movie's Vietnamese village sets were considered so authentic that the army requested they be left when filming ended. They were used for training troops destined for postings in Vietnam.

America's military relished Wayne's support and promotion of their role in keeping American values

Garth at the unveiling of the RAH-66 Comanche helicopter named *The Duke* in honor of John Wayne, on May 13, 1998.

safe, so it's no surprise that as well as receiving a U.S. Congressional Gold Medal mere days before his death in 1979, Duke was also awarded a Presidential Medal of Freedom in June 1980, and a Naval Heritage Award in 1998 for his support of the navy.

That same year Garth Brooks took a day out of his tour of America in order to assist in honoring John Wayne in Washington, on behalf of the U.S. Army. After a guided tour of Arlington National Cemetery, Brooks presented a wreath at the Tomb of the Unknowns and then dedicated a new stealth RAH-66 Comanche helicopter as *The Duke*, in memory of Wayne.

"We've always been the defenders of freedom," said Brooks in his dedication speech, "but in recent times we've also become the peacekeepers for the world. With that goal in mind, I'm proud to be here and dedicate this in memory of John Wayne and what he stood for."

The Oklahoma kid who grew up watching cowboys on TV was, at that time, almost as much an American idol as Wayne had been. Not that Garth would admit as much.

One of Brooks's elementary school friends, Todd Johnson, who also
lived on Yukon Avenue, told Shirley Jinkins of the *Fort Worth Star-
Telegram* in 1993, that Garth was a "well-mannered" kid who loved the
limelight. "Garth was also a ham, he loved attention." Most of those who
remember Garth Brooks's childhood and school days make the point
that there was nothing very special or remarkable about him, though.
At the height of Garthmania, Johnson recalled that young Garth was
"kind of chunky, not really heavy or anything. In the summers we all
lived at the swimming pool. There was no sign, growing up, that any of
this would ever happen." One of Brooks's high school English teachers
remembered him as being nothing out of the ordinary, either. "To me,
Garth was just an average student," she told the *Fort Worth Star-Telegram*
in 1993. However, at home Raymond encouraged a competitive spirit
among his kids, and it meant that Garth was never complacent about any
competitive activity. During his school athletic career Garth always had
to compete with his more talented older brother Kelly. Larry LoBaugh
was principal and a football coach of the school team, the Yukon Millers,
when Garth was at Yukon High. "He wasn't a great football player, but
he had some ability and a lot of heart. He was a team leader and the kids
followed him," he told the *Fort Worth Star-Telegram*.

In 1979, Garth Brooks made it to starting quarterback for the Yukon
Millers, but he kept the job for only half a season. Coach Milt Bassett

told the Woodward.net news site on January 7, 2007, that "Garth was an average college athlete. Yes, I benched him, it was just something that needed to be done." A flawed quarterback perhaps, but Bassett could not find fault with the boy as a human being. "Garth was one of the greatest kids you could ever be around. He was a good kid with a good family," he told Robert Przybylo of NewsOK.com on July 24, 2010.

Interviewing a brand-new music act typically involves some mandatory small talk before jumping into the greatest music reporter cliché question of all time: "What are your musical influences?" When asked, most country music artists at the end of the 1980s neatly trotted out the same old list of tried and trusted musical heroes, from Hank Williams to Dolly Parton, Tammy Wynette, Elvis, and George Jones. Occasionally a more forward-thinking act like Ricky Skaggs or Dwight Yoakam would throw in a Beatles or Rolling Stones reference, but that was about it. Country acts listened to country music. Period.

So Garth Brooks's response to my stock question was something of a shock. He gave me the usual suspects, George Strait, George Jones, and Merle Haggard. But then he spiced things up with some rather unexpected names. "KISS," he said. "Queen, Skynyrd, Led Zeppelin, Billy Joel, James Taylor, Dan Fogelberg, the Eagles."

KISS? Queen? Dan Fogelberg, of all people?!

I must have looked perplexed, because Brooks gave a knowing smile and began to explain. "I'm the youngest kid in my family, so I got to be made aware of all kinds of music through my brothers and sister. They'd bring home and play all kinds of stuff, from Elton John to James Taylor. Then there's the country influence from living in Oklahoma and from my mom and dad. So that's me, singer-songwriter, rock and roll, and country, I guess."

Sarah Crosbie of the *Jeff and Sarah Show* from radio station Q107 in Calgary, spoke to Garth Brooks at a Calgary Stampede news conference in 2012, and asked him about his first rock-and-roll concert memories. He started by recalling that expensive rock shows were price-prohibitive for his family. Not that Colleen and Raymond were keen for their youngest to be exposed to the pleasures of rock and roll, anyway. The first concert his protective parents allowed him to attend was by "Styx, or Kansas, one of those two," he half-recollected. His older brother took him. "My first concert was with Kelly, 'cos they [his parents] knew he would watch out for me and stuff." Good as that show was, it was another heavyweight rock band visiting Oklahoma City that inspired Brooks's eventual career path, though. "My high school sweetheart gave me a surprise; thirteenth row—Freddie Mercury and Queen. That changed my life. I mean, standing on the chair, I have my hands out and screaming out loud and I can hear myself—'this is what I want to do.'"

Brooks later told the reporter that the Queen show was for him "the essence of entertainment." After that, the music bug that started with family entertainment nights continued to grow within Garth Brooks, and he focused more seriously on singing and playing music as he became a teenager, working diligently to master playing his first Gibson acoustic guitar. For his sixteenth birthday he was presented with a banjo, which he similarly plugged away on until he was good enough to play decent bluegrass banjo.

With high school coming to an end along with the 1970s, Garth opted to apply for a place at Oklahoma State University. Kelly was already there on a track scholarship, and the youngest Brooks kid, while never as talented athletically as his brother, scored himself a partial scholarship by throwing the javelin. His major was advertising, not marketing, as critics would mistakenly point to years later, when Brooks was smashing all kinds of sales records.

As with his high school sports efforts, Brooks was known more for his pleasant persona, team ethic, and willingness to give it all he had than any innate athletic talents. His coach, Dick Weis, was candid and to the point when he described his famous student's track prowess to *Country Weekly* on April 1, 1996. "He was adequate. He wasn't outstanding. He wasn't terrible. He'd win some of the smaller meets. He was just a good kid. He came to practice all the time. We never had any problems with him. If he wasn't throwing good, he'd get upset, but that was typical." Brooks agreed with that assessment. It was not his thing, he told the *Country Weekly* correspondent, "It was for the good guys who would eat, sleep, and think javelin. They'd work on it all the time and didn't consider it work. Me, just hauling that damn thing down the runway was work."

Gary Polson was a volunteer coach at the time, and remembered crossing paths with Brooks in an interview with Strengthtech.com: "During the years of my helping out at the track, I got to know Garth Brooks. He is a fine person and always a lot of laughs. Garth competed as a javelin thrower, but was much smaller than most people in this event. As with the other OSU track athletes, what he lacked in talent he made up in effort, spirit, and character. Sometimes I went out to eat with the throwers. Garth held his own at what he called "Power Eating."

It was another javelin coach, Linda Hoisington, who ended Brooks's athletic ambitions and pushed him toward music and show business, instead. Brooks often told the tale while in concert, recounting that at an athletic meeting in Lincoln, Nebraska, he was performing poorly when Coach Hoisington gently suggested he should be doing something else. Although as she recalled, "I don't remember doing this," she continued telling Cezanne McHenry of the Stillwater *NewsPress* in 1992, "but he's told the story several times in concert. He said that I walked up to him and patted him on the shoulder, saying he should get on with what he

was meant to do." Hoisington did remember that Brooks was already an accomplished singer, who "would serenade us on a regular basis. He was always a theatrical showman."

Brooks wasn't shy around campus. He'd sing and play, solo or with others, whenever the chance arose. He was asked to represent his dorm, Iba Hall, in a talent show, which he duly won. He also regularly performed at the student union's Friday night music shows, and he stepped off campus at times, too, entertaining the sick kids at the Stillwater Medical Center as a trio with college pals Dale Pierce and Jim Kelley. They called themselves Dakota Blue.

Dale Pierce told *Oklahoma Today* magazine in January 1993, that "I always knew Garth was going to make it. He and I used to more or less keep everybody up, until they'd kick us out. He always had a stage presence, even just sitting and picking in the living room. He'd be singing in the hall, and people would stop and turn around and look."

When older brother and roommate Kelly graduated from Oklahoma State, Brooks shared accommodation with another music-obsessed student, Ty England. Aside from talking and playing music, conversation between these two turned increasingly to dreams and plans of making it in the recording industry. Brooks recalled those conversations to Westwood One's Tom Rivers in the *Garth Brooks Story* radio special in 1996: "We roomed together at Oklahoma State. And we were sitting up one night, like we always did about three in the morning playing guitars. And we made a pact with each other that someday if we got to do this, we were hopefully going to play together."

It wouldn't be too long before they did.

BILLY JOEL

When Garth Brooks honored singer-songwriter Billy Joel at the Kennedy Center in 2013, he said: "His catalog is so deep, you could have taken the six or seven songs that we did for a tribute to him, wipe them out and put six or seven more Billy Joel songs in there, and I don't think you would notice a difference." Brooks continued, "You'll be stunned if you look up and actually see how many Billy Joel songs you know and that you really loved." It was a Joel song, "Shameless," covered on Brooks's *Ropin' the Wind* album that set Garth apart from his country rivals at the time of its release in 1991. It wasn't originally a country song, but in Brooks's hands it went to #1 around the world, helping the album sell more than 15 million copies globally..

Garth grew up listening to Joel's albums, as did millions of other people who knew a great song with a catchy hook and intelligent lyric when they heard it. Joel hasn't always been the critics' darling, though. Indeed he was often the exact opposite. But "The Piano Man" has outlasted many of his more critically acclaimed contemporaries, and Joel is now rightly regarded as a bona fide chronicler of American life and a pop-and-rock legend. A classically trained New Yorker, Joel started his music career playing in bands, beginning with the Beatles-esque Echoes, then the Hassles, and then the ludicrously named and attired Attila (a heavy-rock duo with long hair who wore animal-skin capes and leather body armor on the cover of their only, eponymously titled album in 1970), before going the solo route in bars and clubs on Long Island. He mixed up his repertoire with songs from artists as eclectic and diverse as Phil Spector, Gershwin, the Beatles, and Fats Domino.

Joel recorded his debut solo album, *Cold Spring Harbor*, for a small record label in 1971, but it failed to cause much of a stir. However, Columbia signed him soon after, and Joel chose to head out west and try his luck in the booming music scene of Los Angeles. Unfortunately, he languished in obscurity there, playing in a piano bar for two years. Still, the experience did result in the classic "Piano Man" song and the LP of the same name (1973). While that album sold well, the follow-up, 1974's *Streetlife Serenade*, didn't do as well, and, frustrated at his apparent lack of traction in the L.A. scene, Joel moved back to the Big Apple and put together the Billy Joel Band, which played on his next record, *Turnstiles* (1976). Some of the tracks had been recorded previously on the West Coast with players from Elton John's band, but Joel wanted a different sound from that made in L.A.—correctly so, as it turned out. The album dealt with Joel's dissatisfaction at life in L.A., and the songs reflected that. The songs were good, especially "Summer," "Highland Falls," "New York State of Mind," and, fittingly, "Say Goodbye to Hollywood."

Joel struck gold (and platinum) with the mega-selling Phil Ramone–produced album *The Stranger* (1977), which contained some of the best-known songs in American pop history of the era, songs like "Just the Way You Are," "Movin' Out (Anthony's Song)," "Only the Good Die Young," and "She's Always a Woman." In the early '80s, stung by barbs from rock critics that he was nothing more than a schmaltzy crooner, Joel toughened up and played some snarling rock and roll. He posed in a rocker's leather jacket on the cover of his hit *Glass Houses* (1980) album. The harder edged approach worked and continued his success, providing him with the hits "You May Be Right," "Don't Ask Me Why," "Sometimes a Fantasy," and the hard-driving "It's Still Rock and Roll to Me."

Billy Joel became a global household name and genuine pop icon in 1983 with *An Innocent Man* and scored his second *Billboard* #1 with "Tell Her About It." Five of the album's tracks made it as Top 30 singles. The collection featured a song that became his biggest smash, the remarkable "Uptown Girl," complete with an MTV-friendly video featuring supermodel Christie Brinkley. She and Joel were married soon after the song became a hit.

Joel continued to have hits, and the 1990s saw him in direct competition with Garth. He was also publicly appreciated and honored for his musical talent. In 1990 he won a Grammy Legend Award, and he was inducted into the Songwriters Hall of Fame in 1992. Membership in the Rock and Roll Hall of Fame followed in 1999. It all added to his success and helped him to sell in excess of 100 million albums.

In November 2014, Joel was given the Gershwin Prize, awarded by the Library of Congress for his lifetime contribution to popular music.

Tony Bennett, John Mellencamp, Josh Groban, Natalie Maines, LeAnn Rimes, and Kevin Spacey joined in the celebrations. Singer-songwriter supreme James Taylor honored him via videotape and correctly identified his old friend with the words, "You are such a treasure, a national treasure."

It's no wonder Garth found inspiration in Billy Joel. He shares Joel's ear for a good phrase, smart tune, and heartfelt sentiment clearly expressed in a song that reaches across social and age ranges.

Garth and Billy Joel performing at the Songwriters Hall of Fame Awards show, New York, 2011.

2

Singing Cowboy

They say that stand-up comedians have the loneliest job in the world. They're all alone up there on stage, with no actors or musicians to share the credit or the blame if things go wrong. Performing as a solo act, playing guitar and singing is similarly daunting for most musicians. The guitar playing has to be spot on, the vocals just so, especially when performing cover versions of well-known songs by much-loved artists. On top of that, the performer also has to entertain. Listening to (and arguably performing) one song played after another with no in-between song banter, jokes, stories, or simple asides can become boring very quickly.

Garth Brooks had to concentrate hard on developing his musician chops and his vocals when he began his career as a singing cowboy. Brooks was always the first to disparage his natural singing talent when starting out, and even after becoming an international star, so he knew better than anyone else how hard he had to work—and how hard he wanted to work anyway—before beginning to make it as a singer. However, when it came to relating to an audience, to drawing them in with a performance and holding their attention, Brooks was a natural. Sure, his skills improved over the years, but even as a novice he exhibited a natural exuberance, a magnetic charm, and gave out such a disarming display of humility mixed with sincerity from the stage that it was clear the man belonged up there.

It so happened of course, that there were lots of solo gigs to be had back then for any competent performer, especially if, like Brooks, they possessed the wherewithal to pick up the phone and make things happen. Some of those gigs even paid OK money for a student—as much as $50 to $100 a night for four or five hours performing. Back then, Brooks's performing style was more low-key than it would later become. When starting out, he'd work his way through an impressive set list of James Taylor, Dan Fogelberg, Neil Young, and Billy Joel tunes, all of which he'd practiced in front of his bedroom mirror before getting in front of small audiences.

Playing songs by those artists made sense to him, because that was what the college market that he was usually playing to wanted to hear at the time—and they were artists Brooks genuinely cared about. The choice of what style of music to play was pretty much determined by the venue and audience. Places like Willie's Saloon, for instance, on the Stillwater strip catered to a hip, young crowd who were essentially conservative, well behaved, well educated, and out on a date (or hoping to be). Other venues Brooks got booked into liked a more country music selection, though. Consequently Garth had more than a few country classics in his set list—which numbered more than three hundred tunes. There were a few by his country music inspiration, George Strait. "I graduated from

ABOVE: George Strait, Garth's
primary country music influence.

PREVIOUS PAGE: Garth
was full of movement, even
when performing with a
static microphone stand.

high school in 1980," he told Tom Rivers for the Westwood One *Garth Brooks Story* radio special in 1996. "And in between my summer year of that and my first year of college at Oklahoma State, I was traveling with my dad to the store. A lady came on the radio as we drove and said, 'here comes a new guy from Texas, I think you're gonna like his sound.' It was George Strait, and from that minute on I knew that I wanted to be a George Strait wannabe, and be just like him."

Brooks may not have been a straight-A student, but he had a gift for memorization, which was a factor that would prove invaluable in the years to come. "You start doing covers, as an artist. That's how you learn about songwriting," Brooks told me during an interview at Nashville's Cockeyed Camel club in the fall of 1988. "Your own songs come later. And the audience in clubs wants to hear the radio hits they know and love. So that's what you give them and slowly you try out an original song during a show." And when Brooks wasn't picking up solo gigs around Stillwater or attending to his advertising studies, he had to work for money. A part-time job at a sports store was appropriate for a student on a javelin scholarship, so that's exactly what Brooks found at Dupree's Sports, close to Wild Willie's at 316 S. Washington Street in Stillwater. The owners had met with Brooks at one of his shows at Wild Willie's, found him engaging, and hooked him up with a job at their store.

Unsurprisingly, he was a good salesman. Brooks was attentive and friendly and remembered names and faces. But even those skills didn't earn him enough money to live well and finance his musical ambitions. So he took on another part-time job, as a bouncer at the Tumbleweed Dance Hall (founded in 1981 as Stillwater Honky-Tonk), where the dance floor was concrete and the music, when not supplied by live bands, came from a couple of old vinyl-spinning record players. That job paid reasonably well, and he managed to avoid any serious physical altercations while he was there. It was a big plus for Garth that the club booked some decent-sized music acts on weekends and brought in a big crowd from around the area, not just locally.

At one such gig on a busy weekend, while carrying out one of his tasks at the Tumbleweed and attempting to end a fight that was taking place in the women's bathroom, Garth made the acquaintance of a young lady who was to leave a big impression on him and the Tumbleweed. He had to help her to remove her fist from a wood panel on the restroom wall, where it had become lodged after she'd thrown a punch and missed the intended target, another female clubber. Brooks was impressed at the feisty blond woman's physical prowess and liked her personality. He offered to drive her home that night, and the attraction proved to be mutual and instant. Her name was Sandy Mahl, later to be Sandy Brooks. "She was amazing," Brooks told me in 1988. "She had the coolest attitude, and we just talked and talked. I knew she was the one."

He may have been in love, but he was never silly. His newfound love affair with Sandy didn't stop Garth from examining his options as an artist—in fact it helped to further those ambitions, with Sandy offering help and support to Garth in his pursuit of a career in music. In 1984 he heard about auditions at Opryland USA, a country music theme park in Nashville, and attended an audition. Already accomplished as a

SOUVENIR PROGRAM

THE GRAND OLE OPRY

ABOVE: The original home of country music from 1943 until 1974, Nashville's Grand Ole Opry at the Ryman Auditorium.

RIGHT: One of Nashville's best-known honky-tonks situated on Broadway, Legends Corner is the kind of place Garth dreamed about playing.

"I had never been out of the state of Oklahoma until I went to Nashville. I was naive and blind to how things work."

GARTH BROOKS

performer, Brooks easily passed the test but ultimately declined the theme park's offer of employment. He did so mainly because, while his mother may have been a show business dreamer, she was determined that Garth would finish his education before trying his luck at something as risky as a career in music—and she had the experience of her own past to offer as reason for that. Raymond Brooks agreed with her, and Opryland was deemed a no-go. Garth didn't stop performing and writing music, though. As he pursued his college degree he continued to play, sing, and listen to new, emerging artists, all the time learning what it takes to become a self-sufficient, successful musical performer.

And as soon as he graduated from Oklahoma State, Brooks revisited his plan to pursue musical ambitions in Nashville. He was confident in his abilities, had a few original tunes in his back pocket, and just knew deep down that Nashville would welcome him with open arms. "I could not wait to get to Nashville," he told me in 1988. "I was convinced doors would open for me. I'd play my songs and I'd be an immediate success. Man, that's not how Nashville is." That first road trip to Nashville didn't quite work out like he had hoped. Brooks was back in Oklahoma within 24 hours, feeling dejected, deflated, and a little sheepish.

While in Nashville on that 1985 trip, Brooks had a meeting at ASCAP, the songwriters collecting and copyright organization, with one of their leading A&R men, Merlin Littlefield, a former radio-promotions man from Texas. Littlefield had moved to Music City from the RCA Records office in Dallas, where he'd worked with, among others, Henry Mancini and Elvis Presley. While in conversation with Littlefield, who had been gracious and curious enough to meet with the newcomer, Garth was hit with a sharp reality check. After some time spent in conversation, they were interrupted by a top Nashville songwriter (recognized by Brooks), who asked Littlefield for a $500 loan. Brooks was dismayed. "After the gentleman left," he told David Huff for *Jam* magazine, "I looked up at Merlin and told him that I made that much money in less than a week where I was from. He looked me straight in the eye and said, 'Then go back home! You aren't ready to make it here!'"

"He was right," Brooks confessed during our first conversation at the Cockeyed Camel in 1988. "I wasn't ready. Maybe I was ready musically but as a human being, man, I just wasn't able to do it on my own, without family and friends from back home. You cannot do this on your own." So he traveled back to Oklahoma, where his first task was to deal with the reactions to his return that folks in Stillwater would have, he wondered. How to explain the debacle of a twenty-three-hour "move" to Nashville? Embarrassed that his "big break" was over so quickly, Brooks hid at his parents' house before venturing out to face people he'd said farewell to. He'd told them he was off in search of country music fame, and yet he'd come back with barely a smell of Nashville on him, let alone any trace of fame. As was his way, though, it didn't take long for Brooks to recover his self-assurance, and he soon stepped back into his old life. He renewed his relationship with Sandy with little trouble, got his old rental house back, and returned to Dupree's Sports to work—and it wasn't long before he was back at familiar venues, playing gigs.

Perhaps Brooks shouldn't have been surprised, and he certainly shouldn't have worried, about the kind of reaction that he'd get from old friends and work pals in Stillwater. "None of them asked what happened," he told Anthony DeCurtis for *Rolling Stone*'s April 1993 issue. "I don't know if it was written all over my face that I didn't want to talk about it, but they didn't say anything. They were really cool." Besides, Brooks didn't have time to be too bashful or embarrassed. He was set on going back to Nashville and making certain that this time, he'd stay.

Local musician Tom Skinner, who knew Brooks from the Stillwater club scene, noted the drive Garth exhibited when he returned to Oklahoma from Nashville. "I've been fortunate in my life to work with many great musicians," Skinner told Tulsaworld.com on January 7, 2015. "But if I ranked them all in order of substance and ability and song-writing talent, Garth would be solidly in the middle somewhere. But if I

ABOVE: New Grass Revival,
the electric bluegrass act that
Garth's band Santa Fe supported
in Stillwater, OK, 1987.

ranked them in order of drive and ambition and goals and how do I get there, Garth is No. 1, and I don't know who is No. 2. He had more of that than anybody I have ever seen."

Working with more determination and spurred on by the memory of that demoralizing trip to Nashville, Garth soon amassed a collection of new songs, from pop to folk to traditional country, and incorporated them into his stage repertoire. The musical mixture was unusually eclectic for his kind of act, but on top of that, he was writing his own songs, which were coming from a dark place inside the Brooks psyche. He explained to Steve Pond of *Playboy* in June 1994 that the deaths of a friend and a roommate left him dealing with mortality at an unusually young age. "I had a buddy from home who said, 'What's the deal with death you got going here?' I said, 'It's really no deal with death. It's just real life to me, and I'm accepting that.' I had a song called 'Lord, Let Me Wake Up Alone' about a guy who goes to bed with a woman for the first time after his wife has died. And he knows that his wife will never be the last woman he's slept with. Now, that's pretty dark and morbid." It was something of a precursor to Brooks' first #1 hit, "Tomorrow Never Comes." That song was inspired by his having watched his by then-wife Sandy sleep and wondering what would happen if he died that night.

As his catalogue of covers and original songs increased, Brooks's ambition grew, and he soon felt that he wanted a bigger musical backing to set his music to. Solo gigs were fine, and he kept all the money, but a band or group could really put across his diverse range of material in the way he imagined it, the way that he heard it in his head. As Brooks would later explain, he had an idea to create a sound that was, "George Strait meets late '70s rock and roll."

Brooks was friendly, or at the least familiar, with most of the players on the Stillwater gig circuit. The Skinner Brothers were well known locally and had been destined for the top, but hadn't found a record deal so far. Tom was a top-notch bass player and with a wife and new baby to support at that time, so regular gig money would be more than handy to him. He was quick to join Garth's project. Later so did his brother Mike, on fiddle and vocals. Garth also persuaded one of the best lead guitar players in the Tulsa area to join, Jed Lindsay. Matt O'Meilia was a rock-and-roll drummer who lived locally and while hesitant at first, since he thought Brooks more country than rock, he was soon charmed enough by Brooks to forget his misgivings about musical style and signed up with the band.

In the spring of 1986 a new, small honky-tonk club opened in Stillwater called Binks. It had no dressing room, but there was a kitchen with enough space to allow performers to change into their stage clothes. The owners needed a solid and versatile house band to entertain their clientele, offer musical backing to visiting performers, and maybe, if they were good enough, play some of their own songs, too. After auditioning plenty of acts from the area, they gave Brooks and the boys the gig. Garth came up with the name Sante Fe for them, and the group was set in motion, debuting at Binks in April of that year.

Working as a house band was just the first step in Brooks's developing plan to make music his career. He kept his Wednesday-night gig at Wild Willie's and set about booking Santa Fe at as many drivable-distance gigs as he could find. They played clubs like the Cimarron and the Tumbleweed Dance Hall (where Brooks had worked as a bouncer) whenever they could, typically picking up as many as five shows a week. These were major-league cubs that were able to book major-league country music acts. so it was that Santa Fe gained some priceless experience playing as the opening act for several of them, getting to meet and talk about music and the business with sisgned artists, including Steve Earle, New Grass Revival, and Dwight Yoakam. All three of those acts were part of a new sound then taking Nashville by storm. New Grass Revival, like Ricky Skaggs a few years before, played contemporary bluegrass. Yoakam went back to country basics with a style rooted in Buck Owens's California sound of the '60s. Earle was a renegade and something of a throwback to the Willie Nelson and Waylon Jennings's outlaw country sound of the mid-'70s.

Garth Brooks watched and listened to them all from the side of the stage after Santa Fe had warmed the audience for them. He listened and learned from them with a keen concentration. Here was proof that country music was changing, that a mixture of rock-and-roll attitude and Western twang could be exciting, new, and successful. Already a devoted fan of George Strait's traditional country, he admired the way Earle and Yoakam brought some rock-and-roll abandon to the proceedings. Could you mix rock and country and truly have the best of both worlds? he wondered. These guys were giving it a good go, and judging from the crowd reaction, they were making it go with a bang.

Most importantly for his own ambitions, Garth liked the way Santa Fe played. Musically they were tight, adaptable, and able to improvise when needed. Drummer Meilia crashed heavily on his drum kit, and the guitar was distinctly heavier than most country twangers sounded. Which was fine and dandy. Brooks had no desire to sound like anyone else. It also seemed to be fine with the crowd at Binks, who had been happy witnesses to Brooks's developing prototype sound when he debuted the band's only original tune at the time, and one of his finest songs, the world-weary "Much Too Young (to Feel this Damn Old)."

Brooks hadn't yet developed the high-energy stage persona in 1986 that he picked up from cowboy star Chris LeDoux, but even back then, with Santa Fe providing a mess of sound to carry him along, Brooks was animated and exuberant on stage. Freed from the physical confines of his solo gigs, Brooks used the whole stage as he determined to emulate his rock-and-roll idols, who'd bring the show to every corner of the room.

Even in his diluted form, Brooks's stagecraft had seemed a radical departure from most country music performers of the day, who typically stood motionless and sang into their microphones—witness any of the television performances to be found on YouTube by Cal Smith, for instance, the writer and performer of one of Garth's favorite country singles, "Country Bumpkin" (1974). Smith stands as if rooted to the spot in front of a straight up-and-down microphone stand, his head hardly moving, not a toe tapping, just his hands moving on the guitar, and then only marginally. The voice and song are fantastic, but the performance is nowhere near as vibrant as anything Garth would do on stage. It wasn't that the songs needed to be enlivened, thought Garth, only the delivery.

It was important to Garth that his way of making music didn't show any disrespect to the old-school country acts that he loved. And Yoakam had shown that you didn't have to either, in order to succeed.

> ## "Then I saw Dwight Yoakam and I said, 'Hey, he ain't just standing there. He's all over the place. We'll pump it up!'"
> ### GARTH BROOKS

LEFT: Dwight Yoakam (right) and Pete Anderson live on stage in 1987, the year that Garth's band played support to them.

RIGHT: Steve Earle, a country music renegade whom Santa Fe also supported in Stillwater, 1987.

GEORGE STRAIT

George Strait (b. May 18, 1952) inducted Garth Brooks into the Country Music Hall of Fame in October 2012. In his acceptance speech Brooks explained why Strait mattered so much to him. He said, "I moved to this town for one reason, and that was to get 'Much Too Young (to Feel This Damn Old)' cut by George Strait. I wanted to be George Strait so bad, man. And I have to say now, twenty years in the business under my own name, thank you very much, I still want to be George Strait so damn bad."

George Strait is a true country music phenomenon. His sales may have been surpassed by the Garth Brooks musical express of the 1990s, but when it comes to longevity, few of the modern era can match Strait. Since the 1980s every one of his 33 LP releases have turned platinum or multi-platinum. He's also had 44 *Billboard* country chart #1s. That's more than any country music artist, ever. And then there are the awards. He's won more CMA and ACM awards and nominations than any other artist in the history of country music. Including Garth.

Unlike Garth Brooks, and in fact in complete contrast to his more exuberant Oklahoman admirer, Strait has always kept it low-key and minimal on stage. There are no theatrics, no pyrotechnics on his performance stage, just George in freshly pressed Wranglers, wearing a cowboy hat and playing an acoustic guitar along to some of the most memorable country music songs of the past three decades, among them "All My Ex's Live in Texas," "Amarillo by Morning," "Carrying Your Love with Me," and "Check Yes or No."

Although a damn fine songwriter, Strait chose to write fewer of his recorded songs over the years, but the success of those recordings proved that he has a knack for picking great songs by new songwriters. In his youth and teen years, Strait's musical taste was initially rock-and-roll flavored, but after hearing Merle Haggard's "Okie from Muskogee" (1969), he was converted to country music.

Strait joined the army in 1972, and when he wasn't protecting his country he was playing in a country band called Rambling Country. On leaving the service in 1975, he took advantage of the G.I. Bill, which allowed him to attend Southwest Texas State University in San Marcos, where he studied agriculture. That was when he joined the remnants of a band called Stoney Ridge as lead singer. They would go on to become the famed Ace in the Hole Band, one of the most acclaimed honky-tonk acts in Texas during the late 1970s.

One of the clubs they played regularly, the Prairie Rose in San Marcos, was owned by a former record company executive named Erv Woolsey. He was so impressed by what he saw in George Strait and the Ace in the Hole Band that when he decided to return to the music business, having taken a job with MCA Records, he set about getting Strait a deal. Woolsey has been Strait's manager ever since, and the Ace in the Hole Band are still George's band.

As Strait told *USA Today*'s Dennis McCafferty on June 21, 2007, "I like people who are loyal to me, and I like to be loyal, too." Perhaps a part of Strait's appeal for Garth can arguably be found in his constancy. Like him, Garth will always be loyal to musicians and live touring crew who work well with him.

Despite three single flops between 1976 and 1979 (released on small independent labels), Woolsey scored Strait a singles deal with major record company MCA, and when his debut for them, "Unwound," went to #5 on the country chart in 1981, an album deal soon followed.

Garth congratulates George Strait on winning Entertainer of the Year at the 48th Academy of Country Music Awards show, Las Vegas, 2013.

George's debut album, *Strait Country*, went Top 30 on the country charts after its release in September 1981. In the years since then, only Elvis and the Beatles have earned more gold and platinum album awards from sales. In the 1990s Strait, like Garth, enjoyed a slew of Top 10 hit LPs and five different #1 albums on the *Billboard* Hot 200 LP charts, as well as regularly topping the country charts.

Despite phenomenal success, George Strait remains something of an enigma in the music business. He has rarely granted interviews, and when he was not recording or on the road, he was typically to be found at his ranch in Texas and competing in roping contests at rodeos. It's possible that the sense of perspective and reality that comes with losing roping contests, in comparison with selling so many records, has kept Strait at the top of the tree for so long. As he told Ray Waddell in the August 16, 2013, *Billboard*, "I've never let the

music business be the only thing in my life....I don't rope much anymore, because it was getting too hard on my back and knees, but that used to be my passion....I love to fish, hunt and play golf. I just love to be outdoors, enjoying God's beautiful creation."

In 2013 Strait became the first country act to be given the prestigious "Legend of Live" award by *Billboard* magazine (for his live touring success). He then chose to announce his retirement from touring after his farewell *The Cowboy Rides Away* tour in 2014. The last concert of that jaunt was recorded for a live album, *The Cowboy Rides Away: Live from AT&T Stadium.* Fittingly, the show broke the venue's attendance record, previously held by the Rolling Stones.

In 2015 Garth Brooks was hoping to at least match George Strait's touring commitment with his first world tour in more than a decade. He will probably always hope to match Strait's haul of awards and commendations, just as he will doubtless always be one of the first people to hear and relish George Strait recordings when they're first released.

With his band's reputation developing nicely, his original material going down well with strangers in the audience, and a life as a musician seeming to be more than attainable, Garth Brooks took a step closer to establishing an adult life on the weekend of May 24, 1986. That was when he married Sandy Mahl in a small family affair. The newlyweds set about getting to really know each other, and later moved into a two-level yellow-and-white-painted house at 227 S. Duck Street in Stillwater. (For anyone interested in a Garth Brooks Stillwater pilgrimage, by the way, there's a plaque on the wall of the porch today that reads, "Garth Brooks Lived Here—1987–1988.")

Later in his career it was often remarked upon how Garth Brooks took a greater-than-usual role in his business affairs. But that would have been no surprise for anyone who'd witnessed the way he managed Santa Fe in Stillwater. Of course, it was his band, so he would be expected to take a lead in making things work, but Brooks took acts of responsibility to another level. He organized the band fund, kept the musicians in order, and tirelessly worked the phones, scoring them gigs and opportunities to gain more exposure on radio and in the local press. It was due to Brooks's persistence and innate sales charm that he won the band a spot on a local news TV show, *A.M. Oklahoma*.

On that first TV appearance, Santa Fe played two songs: Charlie Daniels's "Drinking My Baby Goodbye" and George Strait's "Nobody in His Right Mind." Brooks was affable and witty during the group's short interview section and displayed his business savvy once again by wearing a Dupree's Sports baseball cap throughout. While Brooks consciously and subconsciously formulated his sound, he also wanted Santa Fe to grow into a touring band, and TV exposure would help to get gigs farther afield than just Stillwater. He knew some of his guys were happy playing local shows and making decent amounts of cash to supplement their day jobs, but his reckoning was that if Santa Fe could gradually pick up large-venue gigs in other cities, maybe the band would be enticed to give Nashville a try. Opening up for and pitting their skills against acts like Dwight Yoakam proved to Santa Fe's members that they were absolutely good enough to take things to the next level.

One night at Wild Willie's, drummer Matt O'Meilia later recalled, Brooks brought up the idea of moving Santa Fe to Nashville. In his book, *Garth Brooks: The Road out of Santa Fe* (University of Oklahoma Press, 1996), O'Meilia writes that Brooks asked the band if they would like to get "the hell out of this place." The drummer asked if he meant Willie's, and Brooks replied, "No man, I don't mean Willie's. I'm talkin' about this town, this state. Guys, we gotta start thinking about Nashville."

Thinking wouldn't take them long, but it would ensure that this time when Garth Brooks headed to Tennessee, it would be for good.

3

If at First You Don't Succeed

The baseball great and New York Yankees legend Yogi Berra once said, "You don't have to swing hard to hit a home run. If you got the timing, it'll go." Being a baseball fan, Garth Brooks certainly appreciated the importance of timing. He burst onto the country music and entertainment scene in the late 1980s, and his arrival could not have been better scheduled.

America was feeling more positive by the middle part of the decade than it had in years. A recession had been beaten off, a hard-hitting Republican president had been elected, and by 1983, the U.S. economy was not just stable but had begun a new phase of financial growth. Economic stability was settling in, and, most importantly for the man on the street, the country was enjoying very low inflation rates.

The United States rallied as a nation to host the 1984 Olympic Games in Los Angeles and showed everyone how to put on big, bold, and successful important world events. Significant lifestyle changes were happening for most Americans as cable TV took off and spawned the MTV generation. Many folks were becoming fascinated by the idea of the home computer, a must-have toy/tool that really took off after International Business Machines launched the IBM PC in 1981.

> "When it came to music, I never saw the crowds of people. I just wanted to get my music out there."
>
> GARTH BROOKS

That two-term Republican president who saw the country through most of the 1980s was Ronald Reagan, a B-movie actor turned politician who knew how to talk to people. He was nicknamed the Great Communicator for a reason. Reagan played it simple, talked directly to the American people, and eschewed all airs and graces so often associated with the power elite in American politics. Reagan (in a move later echoed by Garth Brooks) was a self-styled cowboy. He wore the gear, dressed the part, and lived the lifestyle without having any genuine experience of the ranching or rodeo lifestyle (he had played

ABOVE: Garth on the hood of the truck that he used in his move from Oklahoma to Tennessee, in 1988.

PREVIOUS PAGE: Garth's take on the "man in black" look.

many cowboy roles in his former occupation, on screen). It was more the mythology and symbolism of the West, the sense of honor, manners, old-fashioned decency, and self-reliance that Reagan (and later Brooks) latched on to as they developed their personas and images.

Pop and rock music in the 1980s was, for the most part, bright, bold, and colorful, and not only because MTV demanded it. The 24-hour music channel changed all genres of pop music with its hunger for content. Video really did kill some radio stars as the beautiful and telegenic scored points over plain but talented music makers. So in came the pop-metal glam rock of Poison, Guns N' Roses, and Def Leppard, while Elvis Costello, U2, Bruce Springsteen, and the Clash tried to "keep it real." The pop crowd danced and bopped to the phenomenon that was Michael Jackson, as well as Prince, Culture Club, Phil Collins, and new young starlets like Madonna and Whitney Houston.

Garth Brooks's Nashville entrance coincided with a changing of the musical guard. Country music was ready for something, a fusion perhaps of the new traditional sound that had been championed by the likes of George Strait, Ricky Skaggs, the Judds, and Randy Travis, the rocking roots country of Dwight Yoakam, Steve Earle & the Dukes, and the poetic singer-songwriter stylings of maverick artists like Lyle Lovett, k.d. lang, and Nanci Griffith.

Brooks told me in serious tones during our very first conversation that in his opinion, the pop-flavored country boom in the early '80s had left country music in bad shape. He couldn't know the irony in that statement, but in a handful of years Brooks would be accused of selling country music out for the pop dollar. But in his mind, his music was always country. He may perform like a rock star, but the music and vocals were country, through and through.

Country music had been traveling in a pop direction through the 1970s, however. Major artists like Glen Campbell, Olivia Newton-John, and Anne Murray crossed pop with country music in the early part of the decade and sold millions of records in the process. Although there was really nothing new in the fusion of country music and pop, the increasing influence of pop music stylings over traditional country sounds was worrying to the naturally conservative members of Nashville's ruling elite and tastemakers.

BELOW: Charlie Rich, the Country Music Association Entertainer of the Year for 1974, who refused to give John Denver the Entertainer of the Year Award at the 1975 CMA Awards show.

When producers Chet Atkins and Owen Bradley had sweetened country with strings and pop arrangements in the 1960s, they developed what became known as the Nashville Sound and sold millions of records with more sophisticated artists like Jim Reeves, Patsy Cline, and Eddy Arnold. Many of their more traditional-sounding "pop" songs had become international hits. In the middle of the 1970s though, so strong were the concerns of some in the Nashville community that a group of artists started the Association of Country Entertainers (in 1974), designed to somehow halt the seepage of pop sounds and styles into their beloved traditional music. The catalyst proved to be when an Australian pop singer, Olivia Newton-John, beat out American country singers Dolly Parton and Loretta Lynn for the CMA Female Vocalist of the Year award.

The troubled traditionalists, among them Dolly Parton, Bill Anderson, Porter Wagoner, Jim Ed Brown, Dottie West, Faron Young, Conway Twitty, and Barbara Mandrell gathered for an inaugural meeting at the Nashville home of George Jones and Tammy Wynette. Their foremost goal was to ensure that country radio maintained a fair balance between traditional and pop-country artists on their playlists. They also sought to get a valid representation of traditional artists on the CMA board of directors.

The traditionalists lobbied within the business for the most part, and while an artist might make a passing remark in interview about how pop music and country didn't really work, there was no big public statement of dissent by the old guard until the 1975 CMA Awards show. Charlie Rich, as the reigning CMA Entertainer of the Year, was tasked with reading the recipient of the biggest prize in country music. John Denver's name was on the card for 1975 Entertainer of the Year, and on reading it to himself, with a flourish Charlie Rich lit the card on fire with a cigarette lighter and grinned as he aimed the flaming card toward the cameras.

However, country music, like any other, catered to the widest possible audience, and despite their misgivings, some prominent ACE artists, Barbara Mandrell and Dolly Parton in particular, opted to join the pop country movement instead of trying to kill it. Dolly Parton, one of the most authentic country voices the genre has ever known, went truly pop in 1977, with her mainstream *Billboard* Hot 100 smash, "Here You Come Again." Barbara Mandrell launched a popular variety show TV career on the back of her 1979 pop country hit "(If Loving You Is Wrong) I Don't Want to Be Right."

The box-office smash movie starring John Travolta and Debra Winger, *Urban Cowboy* (1980), with its hit-filled soundtrack, did for country music what Travolta's previous two hit movies had done for disco (*Saturday Night Fever*, 1977) and old-time rock and roll (*Grease*, 1978), and ushered in a temporary trend for country music and fashion across America. It was a slushy soap opera of a movie, but the film was saved by guest appearances from real-deal country acts Mickey Gilley, Johnny Lee, and the Charlie Daniels Band. The soundtrack included Johnny Lee's massive hit "Lookin' for Love (in All the Wrong Places)," Alabama's harmonious ballad "The Closer You Get," and Barbara Mandrell's feisty musical claim that she was "Country When Country Wasn't Cool."

Thousands of people across America tried line dancing and donned Wranglers and cowboy boots, as the country craze swept from coast to coast. But it proved to be more of a flavor-of-the-month fashion statement than anything substantial, and the music that surfaced as a result of its success came and went on the pop charts pretty quickly.

Garth Brooks wasn't taken in by it, as he told *Playboy*'s Steve Pond in 1994. "The *Urban Cowboy* thing was more money-driven. It was a fad, and it was almost the death of country music. If it weren't for people like George Strait, Ricky Skaggs, and Reba McEntire, I'm not sure country would've held on until the guys like Randy Travis came and country music in its purest form was saved."

The saving of country music was the very reason I met the young Garth Brooks in the first place. That interview and club gig in West Nashville in the fall of 1988 was just one part of a research trip I'd made to Music City to gather background material for a book about what was then referred to as New Country.

Country music had prospered in the early 1980s, thanks to the previously referenced *Urban Cowboy*–led boom, but the artists who surfaced and the style they performed was syrupy and soft, a much-diluted version of the music played by Merle Haggard, Loretta Lynn, and George Jones. Once the *Urban Cowboy* scene dissipated, country radio was left with a bland pop sound, and listeners fell away quickly. Record sales across the country genre were down in the mid-1980s, and some critics wondered if country music had any real future.

It was a one-time folk singer, Emmylou Harris (b. 1947), who really started the process of saving country music from itself. Harris first became known to country and rock fans through her duet work with the country-rock pioneer and notorious heroin addict Gram Parsons (b. 1946). Parsons had a vision for blending country music (the authentic and rootsy George Jones/Bill Monroe variety) with rock and roll in the 1960s. He succeeded to a degree, with some fine records made with his Flying Burrito Brothers. Parsons was also responsible for getting the Byrds to record *Sweetheart of the Rodeo* (1968), which led to the band and Parsons making a disastrous appearance at the Grand Ole Opry in 1968, at which they were jeered off stage. Proclaiming to make "real American music," for a time he resided at Keith Richards's chateau in France and is credited for inspiring the Stones's country-tinged recordings, including "Wild Horses" (first recorded by the Flying Burrito Brothers). Parsons recorded two solo albums featuring Emmylou in the early 1970s—both *GP* (1973) and *Grievous Angel* (1974) featured Harris prominently, and while

Hard hat days
and honky-tonk nights.

JOHN TRAVOLTA
URBAN
COWBOY

PARAMOUNT PICTURES PRESENTS A ROBERT EVANS/IRVING AZOFF PRODUCTION
A JAMES BRIDGES FILM JOHN TRAVOLTA "URBAN COWBOY" ALSO STARRING DEBRA WINGER
EXECUTIVE PRODUCER C.O. ERICKSON BASED UPON THE STORY BY AARON LATHAM
SCREENPLAY BY JAMES BRIDGES AND AARON LATHAM PRODUCED BY ROBERT EVANS & IRVING AZOFF
DIRECTED BY JAMES BRIDGES PANAVISION®
A PARAMOUNT PICTURE
PG PARENTAL GUIDANCE SUGGESTED
SOME MATERIAL MAY NOT BE SUITABLE FOR CHILDREN
©MCMLXXX BY PARAMOUNT PICTURES CORPORATION
ALL RIGHTS RESERVED

**ABOVE: The movie that turned
the whole of America on to
cowboy hats, country music,
and line dancing in 1980.**

they failed to sell at the time, they have, since Parsons's untimely death at twenty-six in 1973, become cult classics. They did, however, launch Harris on her career, and she continued his legacy. Along with Linda Ronstadt and the Eagles, she took Parsons's vision and turned country rock into a hugely commercial sound throughout the 1970s. In 1975, Harris hired a young Texan singer-songwriter named Rodney Crowell to play guitar and sing with her Hot Band. He would go on to establish a career that came close to matching rock music with country, and he became Johnny Cash's son-in-law when he married Cash's daughter, Rosanne.

By the next decade Emmylou was looking back to her folk and country roots and recorded her seminal *Roses in the Snow* album in 1980. It was a beautiful record, and its folksy, bluegrass-influenced sound was anathema to the country pop on the radio. Bluegrass musician Ricky

ABOVE: Reba McEntire, one of the first women to redefine country music's expectations for female performers in the late 1980s.

Skaggs (b. 1954) played a significant role in the album's back-to-basics sound, and between them, Skaggs and Harris reminded Nashville's movers and shakers and a host of artists that country music had deep and sincere roots. The tide was ready to turn. Skaggs's impact in contributing near-perfect bluegrass-style guitar, banjo, fiddle, mandolin, and high haunting harmony vocals was significant. The album's critical reception gave Skaggs the confidence to launch his own solo career along similar lines. Over the next few years he brought a genuine folksy mountain sound back to the mainstream country radio mix.

Skaggs told me in 2011 that there was a genuine feeling among country music players around the end of the 1970s that the music was losing sight of its roots. "My vision, after working with Emmylou, was to mix old-time mountain instrumentation with high-quality, state-of-the-art production values in Nashville." Clearly the one-time bluegrass prodigy was on to something, since his music reverberated around Music City, and Skaggs was voted the year's best male vocalist in 1982. It was a pat-on-the-back reward for one of the finest records of the decade, *Waitin' for the Sun to Shine* and its two #1 country hits, "Cryin' My Heart Out over You" and "I Don't Care." Two years later, Skaggs's frantic cover of Bill Monroe's classic bluegrass tune "Uncle Pen" became his ninth #1 country single—and turned Garth Brooks into a fan of Ricky Skaggs. The two men became firm friends soon after Garth moved to Nashville, following an introduction by their mutual pal, Steve Wariner.

Raised on an Oklahoma cattle ranch, Reba McEntire (b. 1955) was singing in a country band while in high school, and had a reputation as a country torch singer when she signed to Mercury Records in 1978. Her first albums were strong but very pop influenced. However, they were not the kind of records she wanted to make or, indeed, listen to. She moved to MCA Records in 1984, and attempted to take the traditional route herself. Despite switching producers mid-recording, her first MCA album, *Just a Little Love* (1984) turned out sounding as much pop as it did country. Fortunately for her though, a new label head arrived at MCA that same year, and the always forward-thinking Jimmy Bowen backed her to the hilt. Turning to her record collection for inspiration, McEntire turned in an album of old songs done in her own way, which was more traditional country than it was pop. When, in 1984, *My Kind of Country* came out to rapturous critical and commercial reception, it made her many new fans and among them was Garth Brooks. Five years later, Reba was one of Garth's biggest supporters in Nashville. "There are lots of artists who can sing but who can't impart the emotion and personality that make an entertainer shine," she told *People* magazine in 1989, before adding that, "Garth pulls it off."

Jimmy Bowen (b. 1936) is a legendary figure in country music, loved by some, but not by all. He grew up in Texas and had a couple of minor rockabilly hits as a singer in 1961 and 1962, before realizing that a career behind the recording console was a safer long-term bet than one in front of the microphone. Bowen moved to L.A. and as a young maverick record producer was hired by Frank Sinatra to work at his nascent label, Reprise Records, where Bowen oversaw some of the then hugely successful Rat Pack's biggest-selling records (including those by Dean Martin and Sammy Davis Jr.). He is credited with introducing Nancy Sinatra to Lee Hazelwood and so sparking a unique and lucrative musical pairing.

In 1968, Bowen started a successful independent label in Los Angeles called Amos Records. Demonstrating a great ear for talent, at one time he had the future Eagles Glenn Frey and Don Henley signed as solo artists.

GEORGE JONES

After George Jones (September 12, 1931–April 26, 2013) passed away, Garth Brooks reminisced to *Billboard*'s Melinda Newman about the time they recorded a duet in 2001, on "Beer Run (B Double E Double Are You In?)." Brooks said, "I think I can describe that day: it was the least I've ever been pissed off at getting out-sung. It was an honor to get my ass kicked that day."

George Jones was so much more than a powerhouse singer, though. He was an innovator and a vocal stylist, often mimicked and never matched. More than that he was an icon, a maverick who refused to conform and was tabloid fodder from almost the day after his first hit single, "Why Baby Why," in 1955. Following his marriage to Tammy Wynette in 1969, the pair became Nashville's own version of Liz Taylor and Richard Burton, their every fight, reconciliation, and public show of disharmony making headlines across the Bible Belt. However, more importantly, Jones sang some timeless country classics, namely, "White Lightning," "She Thinks I Still Care," "Tender Years," and "He Stopped Loving Her Today."

George Jones grew up in post–Great Depression Texas, listening to Roy Acuff and Hank Williams and the rest of the Grand Ole Opry cast on WSM radio. Enamored with music before he was ten years old, Jones played guitar and sang on street corners as a young kid in Beaumont, collecting pennies and dimes for food and shoes. He embarked on a professional music career with Starday Records in 1953, soon after being discharged from the Marines, with whom he served in California.

His first single release failed to make much of an impact, but in 1955, he reached #4 on the *Billboard* country chart with the near-rockabilly "Why Baby Why."

It was the first of a phenomenal 166 singles to make the charts in a long and always eventful career. Jones was the biggest star and the male face of country music in the 1960s and early '70s, inevitably influencing and inspiring every new male singer who came along.

At the end of the 1960s, his career and personal life took a dramatic turn when he met fellow Nashville singing star Tammy Wynette. They married after a tempestuous courtship—they were both already married, George to his second wife, Tammy her first husband—and it set the tone of their six-year union. Through the early part of the 1970s, the couple were the undisputed king and queen of country music duets with a series of hits that included "Take Me," "We Go Together," "We're Gonna Hold On," and "We Loved It Away." "Golden Ring" was recorded after their divorce in 1975, but remains one of the greatest county music duets of all time.

Their not-so-private life appeared to be the stuff of a country songwriter's imagination. George's addiction to various intoxicating substances led to his becoming notorious for canceling live appearances at very short notice (earning him the sobriquet No-Show Jones), and his tendencies to throw a fist at anyone who argued with him while he was on a bender added to his reputation as a difficult star to follow. Stories began to proliferate concerning the fights that George and Tammy got into at their palatial home. Sadly, unlike June Carter Cash, who managed to calm the demons in her country music legend husband Johnny, Wynette was unable to coax George Jones past his addiction to alcohol. So arguments and fights, including many in public, kept the pair in the limelight but took their toll on both artists.

Jones kept recording in the 1980s, though, if not at the pace of the '60s and '70s, and he even remained relevant through the 1990s. He was voted into the prestigious Country Music Hall of Fame in 1992 and in 1999, scored a final Top 30 hit with the remarkably apt "Choices." It also won him a Grammy. Like all of his recordings, Jones kept his country music traditional, and ultimately it was that resolute purity that won him so many fans.

In 2012, a host of top artists were slated to play with Jones at a special tribute concert planned for Nashville in November 2013, including Garth Brooks, Kid Rock, and the Charlie Daniels Band. He even had one of the Rolling Stones, Keith Richards, a long-time fan, lined up to perform. The rock icon told the *Tennessean* newspaper that he planned to be there, "by hook or by crook." Sadly their sell-out tribute show didn't feature

Jones. He died a little more than six months prior to the date, at Vanderbilt University Medical Center in Nashville. He had been suffering with fever and irregular blood pressure before finally succumbing to the one excuse for a no-show that nobody could argue with.

But a host of stars did play the tribute concert to him. Artists who showed up included Blake Shelton, Miranda Lambert, Brad Paisley, Vince Gill, Emmylou Harris, Kid Rock, Alan Jackson, and Eric Church. It was left to Garth Brooks and his wife, Trisha Yearwood, to bring the house down with a touching and note-perfect rendition of the Jones and Wynette hit "Take Me."

Garth and George Jones performing "Beer Run" at the 35th Academy of Country Music Awards show, Nashville, 2001.

ABOVE: Jimmy Bowen (left) with Glen Campbell, signing a contract to record with MCA in 1987. Shortly after, Bowen joined Capitol and helped Garth build his career.

When he arrived in Nashville in 1971, Bowen was shocked at the parochial way much of the industry did business. Unafraid to rock the boat, he upset the good ol' boy network on several occasions. He reputedly fired everyone when he arrived at MCA except the executive assistant and the mailman, for instance. "When I ran a company, I always told them I was a benevolent dictator. Democracies are too slow for business," he told the *Nashville Scene*'s Beverly Keel in 1997, as he talked up his memoirs. "If you are going to move and get a lot done in a short period of time and be successful in business, you've got to make decisions, act and move forward. . . . The fact that you are getting it done, you know going in that you're going to make mistakes—like passing on a great act, well, so you did. It was also great what we did do."

One act he passed on while at MCA, though, was a young singer from Yukon, Oklahoma, named Brooks. It proved to be something that Bowen would put very much right when he took over Capitol however, just as Garth Brooks scored his first hit. Bowen was appreciative of artists who knew what they wanted and how to get it, as he'd proved with Reba.

The reason Bowen let Reba McEntire have musical control over *My Kind of Country*, he stated in his 1997 autobiography, *Rough Mix* (Simon & Schuster, 1997), was that Reba, until that album, had never been allowed to be "country." "No one knew it," he wrote, "but Reba was on the cutting edge of the New Traditional movement." By allowing her artistic freedom to make music, Bowen launched Reba to superstardom. The album gave her two #1 country singles, "How Blue" and "Somebody Should Leave."

> # "True country music is honesty, sincerity, and real life to the hilt."
> ### GARTH BROOKS

Bowen adopted a similar philosophy of allowing his artists more, rather than less, creative control with another traditional act, George Strait (b. 1952). Strait's chiseled good looks and clean-cut persona allied with a traditional Texas honky-tonk sound had matched Ricky Skaggs in bringing traditional country back to the mainstream. His debut album, *Strait Country*, complete with the single "Unwound," which so affected Garth Brooks, appeared in 1981 on Bowen's MCA Records. Bowen understood that Strait was Western through and through, and toning it down in order to appeal to a wider audience never entered his mind, no more than it did Strait's.

Jimmy Bowen allowed Strait more control in his sound and ramped up promotion and marketing efforts for 1984's *Does Fort Worth Ever Cross Your Mind* album. That album proved to offer more of the same kind of music and delivery, but was better played and more powerfully presented than before. Renowned critic Robert Christgau was impressed with the album's integrity, writing, "what I get from his best album and

song selection to date is a convincing, tuneful show of honesty. B+." The album went platinum (one million copies sold) and won the CMA award for Album of the Year.

Once the New Country movement took hold in Nashville and on country music radio, more artists surfaced who were playing a minimalist country style, and by doing so they encouraged a younger audience to tune in and check it out. Naturally, every major label wanted New Country artists. RCA Records recognized the acoustic purity of mother-and-daughter duo the Judds. Theirs was a classic country music rags-to-riches tale. Naomi (b. 1946, real name Diana) Judd was raised in Kentucky but moved to California with daughter Wynonna (b. 1964, originally christened Christina) for a short-term marriage. A second daughter, Ashley, followed (in 1968) but when the marriage broke down Naomi brought her family back to Kentucky and studied to be a nurse.

LEFT: Early days in Nashville.
Garth is introduced to
superstars Wynonna (center)
and Naomi Judd by his first
and hugely influential PR
agent, Pam Lewis (left).

After finishing her degree on the West Coast, and aware that Wynonna had a rare vocal talent, the Judds moved to Nashville. Ashley had rare good looks, and after graduating from the University of Kentucky, she became an actress and Hollywood star. Taking music seriously, the mother-and-daughter act produced demo cassettes and made a few appearances on a local morning TV show. Producer Brent Maher met Naomi Judd when she was nursing his daughter in the hospital, following a car crash. Maher was fascinated by the Judds' vocal blend and Appalachian mountain style and eventually got them a live audition with RCA records. So powerful was the sound that they were signed there and then, and a young PR agent named Pam Lewis became their champion.

The Judds' second single, "Mama He's Crazy," made them household names and scored them a Grammy. Their debut album, *Why Not Me* (1984), became a classic of new traditional music and spoke to a new generation of female country music fans. Pam Lewis would later introduce Garth to the Judds, and thereafter they became firm friends.

Warner Brothers Records' contribution to the New Traditionalist movement came in the shape of a young singer who sounded like a world-weary veteran, Randy Travis (b. 1959). Travis was classified as being too country for radio by all the major labels in Nashville in the early 1980s. His wife and manager, Lib Hatcher, was determined to break through the bias, though. She took a job as manager of the Nashville Palace club and found Travis (then known as Randy Ray) a job as a short-order cook and part-time singer. Hatcher recorded some of his back-to-basics songs live from the sound board at the venue, and with Travis's rich, booming vocals much in evidence, finally swung a deal with Warner Brothers. Randy Ray officially became Randy Travis, and his second single "1982," went Top 10 in 1986. On the back of that success Warner Brothers reissued Travis's first single, "On the Other Hand," and it went to #1 the second time around. His debut album, *Storms of Life* (1986), was proof that a new traditional sound of country music had a sizeable fan base, and it sold in excess of four million copies. Travis won the Academy of Country Music award for Best Country Newcomer in 1986.

Garth Brooks had, of course, been fortunate enough to open for another New Country stalwart, Kentucky-raised but California-sounding Dwight Yoakam (b. 1956), in 1987. Yoakam reinvented the Buck Owens/Bakersfield sound and headed to Nashville to find fame and fortune in the late 1970s. Like Travis, Yoakam was initially rejected by Nashville for sounding "too country." Undeterred, he relocated to Los Angeles, where he avoided the country bars and instead assembled a loud rocking band and played rock-and-roll venues. Alongside punk and rock acts like X, the Blasters, and Los Lobos, Yoakam did what he planned all along, and captured the maverick spirit of Hank Williams, wrapping it in the upbeat honky-tonk sound of Buck Owens. There was nothing pop or crossover about Yoakam. His debut album, *Guitars, Cadillacs, Etc.* (1986), was critically acclaimed, and while it and the follow-up album, *Hillbilly Deluxe* (1987), sold in fewer numbers than Randy Travis's and Reba McEntire's releases, Yoakam played a massive role in attracting young rock-and-roll fans to a genre they may have otherwise avoided because of a country music prejudice.

Although Nashville might have been perfectly primed for Garth Brooks's relocation in 1987, Brooks was taking no chances this time. One thing he'd learned from that previous, embarrassingly quick trip was that he couldn't make it on his own. He needed the support that his wife, Sandy, and his band provided.

Aside from Garth Brooks's newfound team ethic, his intuitive ability to sort the genuine from the phonies also played a significant part in his propulsion to the top. He gravitated toward people with real talent and whose contacts were kosher and legitimate. That was absolutely key in Nashville in the late 1980s. Music Row was, and perhaps remains, riddled with con men and scam artists ready to take any new act that comes to town for every penny they have. Producers and promoters would find singers in Nashville's many songwriting rooms, feed the out-of-towners some hot air about their talent, and then ask for serious amounts of money to get them started. They could even get them on the radio and on the charts, they promised. And often they did, except the chart they used to impress their musical prey was corruptly compiled.

The chart-rigging scandal was exposed in the media in March 1989, following the murder of Kevin Hughes by Richard D'Antonio on 16th Avenue South, in the heart of Nashville's Music Row area. Hughes had refused to follow the practice of his predecessor and fix the charts for money. Hughes replaced D'Antonio as head of the country charts for *Cashbox* magazine, which was then a struggling but once important trade publication.

By printing its own independent country music chart, the magazine was able to give attention to acts not significant enough to figure on the more prestigious and larger *Billboard* chart, which was compiled using record sales and radio plays gathered from impeccable sources around the country. *Cashbox* employed Hughes to replace D'Antonio to track radio plays for their chart compilation because they knew he was honest and unlikely to take the same kind of bribes that his predecessor had.

At the time of Hughes's death he was involved in trying to prevent some unscrupulous record promoters from buying their artists' places on the *Cashbox* chart. Hughes threatened to expose D'Antonio for taking money from major promo man Chuck Dixon (whose funeral in Philadelphia in 2001 was attended by several members of a prominent crime family) in return for favorable showings for certain acts, usually at the expense of more legitimate contenders for the chart placing. The

practice had been going on for years—Dixon openly boasted about
the control he had over *Cashbox*—until Hughes took it upon himself to
straighten out the charts. When he refused to take money from Dixon,
Hughes and a friend, Sammy Sadler, were gunned down on leaving a
recording studio. Hughes was shot several times, Sadler just once (he was
considered collateral damage). It took the authorities until 2003 to finally
convict D'Antonio of first-degree murder and intent to commit second-
degree murder (of Sadler).

Brooks fortunately moved in very different circles when he arrived in
Nashville, green but not wholly ignorant of the workings of the recording
industry. It was something he'd been primed for by his mother, Colleen.
"I was lucky. I had a mother who had been signed to a recording contract.
She understood the music business and that it could be a tough place.
She drilled it into me to be careful and not believe everything I was told,"
Brooks told me in 1988.

The first Nashville contact Brooks leaned on for advice and help was a
fellow Stillwater musician named Bob Childers. Before bringing his wife

LEFT: Every male country
performer in Nashville in
the late 1980s had to own a
tuxedo and a best Stetson.

and band along for the ride, Brooks and Santa Fe guitarist Jed Lindsay
visited Nashville on several occasions, ostensibly scouting places to live
but also meeting songwriters at some of Nashville's popular songwriter
nights. Bob Childers (b. 1946) was more established as an artist than
Brooks. Recognized now as a pioneering voice in the Red Dirt sound,
a particularly Oklahoman fusion of country folk and blues, Childers
presented the quieter, more intimate singer-songwriter aspect of Brooks's
musical taste. Equally as much a fan of Woody Guthrie as he was of
Merle Haggard, Childers (who died in 2008), was a poet with a guitar.
Like Townes Van Zandt, Steve Earle, Lyle Lovett, and Guy Clark, he
instinctively drew on American roots music as he told stories and painted
pictures in words during sometimes delicate and often gritty three-
minute musical vignettes.

Childers recorded his first album, *I Ain't No Jukebox* in 1979, in
Stillwater, Oklahoma, aided and abetted by fellow Oklahoma songsmith
Jimmy LaFave. The album did well, established Childers as a folkie-
meets-country talent, and, along with LaFave, set the Red Dirt sound
into motion. In 1986 he tried his hand at the big leagues and headed
east to Nashville.

Childers lived near Music Row in Nashville, the hub of the business
that Brooks wanted so much to be a part of. Childers was having a tough
time in Music City, though. His kids were back in Oklahoma, and he
was missing them. When he received a call from Jed Lindsay that he
and Garth would appreciate it if they could crash at his apartment for
a while, Childers figured the company and distraction might help him
feel less homesick. Lindsay had a sterling reputation within Stillwater
musician circles and the fact that he was working with this new singer-
songwriter gave Childers confidence that Brooks could be the real deal.
Even before they arrived at his small, two-bedroom apartment, Childers
had made some introductory calls on Brooks's behalf. One of them was to
a songwriter friend named Stephanie Brown. He thought she'd be a good
person for Garth Brooks to know.

The second night that Brooks stayed with Bob Childers he went to
a club and met up with Stephanie. Brooks told CNN's Larry King on
September 27, 1999, "I believe there are angels that are sent into our life.
One of those angels for me was a lady named Stephanie Brown. I met her
the second or third night I was in Nashville, at a writers' night, and she
said there was this gentleman, and she thought the two of us would get
along great. His name was Bob Doyle."

Doyle would become the catalyst in building Brooks's dream team—
right after Garth had helped Sandy and his family of musicians get
settled into a house he had scouted in Hendersonville, a small town a few
miles north of Nashville.

4
The Real Deal

There's more to Nashville than music. More than half of America's healthcare business is located there, for instance, while religious publishing and a massive evangelical Christian business network dwarf the music business. Thomas Nelson, the biggest Bible publishing company in the world, is headquartered in Nashville. As is the United Methodist Publishing House, the largest church-owned and-operated publishing and printing operation to be found anywhere. No wonder Nashville been tagged "the buckle of the Bible Belt."

But what makes Nashville very different from similar-sized predominately conservative, Protestant Evangelical cities in the South is the music industry. Ever since the music business made itself home in Nashville, the city has seen an influx of writers, artists, eccentrics, hipsters, and political mavericks rubbing shoulders with the region's

more conservative community. Some of the best art to surface from Nashville in the past sixty years has been a result of that eternal conflict between the Bible and the bottle.

Nashville's music story dates back to the 1920s, and the development of a 50,000-watt AM radio station. WSM is now regarded as one of the great country stations, but it started life as a promotional vehicle for the Nashville-based National Life and Accident Insurance Company. They used the slogan "We Shield Millions," or WSM, and produced a one-hour country music show that quickly expanded into a four-hour hillbilly variety show during the Depression years of the 1930s. The radio show tried several Nashville venues as it grew in popularity, and thousands of country music fans drove into Nashville for weekend trips to see and hear the stars of the day. Eventually, on June 5, 1943, the Opry moved to its most famous location, the Ryman Auditorium in downtown Nashville. It was at the Ryman Auditorium that country music history in its first classic era was created. This was the time of Bill Monroe and his invention of a new genre, bluegrass. In 1949, Hank Williams, perhaps the greatest country music artist of all time, played an unheard of six encores of "Lovesick Blues" for the delirious audience.

Country music artists traveled from all over America to be on the radio show, and fans flocked in from neighboring states as well, to hear the music and watch the stars in action in downtown Nashville. RCA Victor carried out some recording in Nashville in the 1920s, but it was the WSM radio engineers, perfecting their recording techniques, that led to Nashville developing as a recording center for country, and later rock and roll and pop music.

Music Row, which is located around 16th, 17th, and 18th Avenues South, really began in the 1950s when record producers Owen and Harold Bradley built the Quonset studio that gave birth to the string heavy Nashville Sound of the late 1950s and early 1960s. Singers like Eddy Arnold, Jim Reeves, and Patsy Cline enjoyed such great commercial success recording in Nashville that more and more musicians realized that Nashville would be ideal for their needs, too.

Elvis Presley recorded for a while at RCA's famous Studio B, and following his superstar name and reputation, hundreds of studios and music-business companies burst on the Music Row scene, many of them located in minimally converted rustic A-frame wooden houses that made up the residential streets around the 16th Avenue South area.

Country legend Roy Acuff and songwriter Fred Rose, frustrated at seeing so many fellow artists taken advantage of by unscrupulous music publishing houses, started their own, calling it simply Acuff-Rose. With their knowledge of the industry, and trusted by fellow musicians, success soon followed and Acuff-Rose inspired the music publishing business to set up shop in Nashville. And then, with Music Row building a reputation for songs and recording, literally thousands of hopeful artists and writers began the trek to Music City, as it swiftly came to be known.

Nashville settled in as America's third most important recording city after New York and Los Angeles in the 1960s, but it was the songwriting community that made Nashville different. As Nashville's recordings under producer Chet Atkins's lead became increasingly polished and orchestrated though the 1960s, so the wave of raw, back-to-basics songwriters emerged, from Harlan "Three Chords and the Truth" Howard to John Hartford, Mickey Newbury, Willie Nelson, and Kris Kristofferson. They connected with country music's down-home roots and rediscovered the power and beauty of raw, cheating-and-drinking songs. And it was life reflecting art as the writers plied their trade over cocktails at musician-friendly bars, like the Tally Ho Bar, Tootsies, and the Kountry Korner Tavern.

Garth Brooks had not found Nashville a particularly hospitable city when he made his first twenty-three-hour visit, but that revealed his unrealistic expectations of being embraced as a future star without first paying any dues. Indeed, there's an unwritten two-year rule followed by country music record labels in Nashville, which says that a new artist has only proven themselves to have the guts and stamina for a recording career after they've spent two years in the city, trying to establish themselves and get a break.

> "In between where you are and where you want to be is a sea of reasons why you can't get here."
>
> GARTH BROOKS

However, Nashville in 1987 was a remarkably friendly and easygoing city, even though it was on the cusp of major change in both economic and cultural terms. Nashville in the latter part of the 1980s was a city about to change. The free-flowing, overtly down-home, friendly, and bar-driven variety of music would morph into a more polished and professional style as people started drinking wine instead of beer, and as record company execs and some artists traded sensible sedans or

pick-up trucks for Mercedes and BMW sports cars. Music types began frequenting more upscale lunch and dinner establishments, like Arthur's restaurant in Union Station Hotel or the exclusive Italian joint Valentino's on West End, which was much loved by executives for a lunchtime rendezvous or two. But songwriters still chose to congregate in bars and clubs. As singer-songwriter legend Guy Clark once told me, "lunch is the most important part of the day for a Nashville songwriter." Lunch, of course fueled by alcohol, would often run into dinner—and maybe even breakfast—as the songwriters soaked in the atmosphere, seeking and often finding that creative spark in their surroundings. These guys weren't college-educated music biz wannabes, trained in the art of verse construction and where to place the song's hook by professors and guest writers in seminars. These were regular guys, often uneducated, but with a gift for wordplay, a knack for finding a hummable melody and a sense of working people's reality. Slowly, Nashville became more corporate, with songs written on beer-stained napkins at Bobby's Idle Hour hole-in-the-wall bar on Music Row being replaced by tunes written by committee

in cozy, upscale writers rooms in air-conditioned, pleasantly fragranced publishing houses on the Row.

And the writers, the great writers, were visible and accessible. A new writer in town could actually meet the legends by being smart and visiting the right places at the right time. The great Harlan Howard, who wrote hits in the '60s for Buck Owens and others, could be found on a regular basis eating his breakfast at Maude's Courtyard on Broadway. Ireland's restaurant around the corner was popular with established stars like Chet Atkins and Ray Stevens.

In the late 1980s, right before Nashville got rich and went professional, global, and slick (mostly because of Brooks's phenomenal and unparalleled success, it has to be noted) the city was a perfect storm of the best of the old-school writer–artist hospitality combined with a newer, more organized and corporate community that would make a few people rich beyond their craziest dreams. For a charismatic and savvy people-person like Garth, the Nashville community would prove perfect for his needs, once he had settled in and prepared his career strategy.

Garth soon found a house to rent that was big enough for him and Sandy, plus the rest of the band and their families as well, in 1987. It was a modest-looking red brick family home with five bedrooms and just enough space, hopefully, for the Stillwater brood to survive long enough for Garth and the band to make it big in Nashville.

The house was situated in Hendersonville, a small town that was home to several country music stars. Johnny Cash and Ricky Skaggs lived there, although their neighbor, country crooner Conway Twitty, outdid them all in flamboyance with his glitzy, sprawling, outsized mansion and museum complex named, appropriately, Twitty City.

Hendersonville is some ten miles north of Nashville, which meant the rent was affordable for a group of musicians with part-time day jobs. Some of the guys in Santa Fe worked shifts at Wal-Mart, others at gas stations and apartment complexes. Brooks lucked out, though. His retail sales experience in the sports store back home in Oklahoma scored him a management position at a cowboy boot shop. As manager he was able to hire his wife, too, which proved useful when he needed to sneak out for a music business meeting.

Country singer Ken Mellons, who cut several hits in the 1990s, first encountered the young Garth Brooks eagerly helping customers pick a pair of boots at Cowtown Boots in Rivergate Mall. It was a few miles north of downtown Nashville and close to their house in Hendersonville.

Mellons reminisced to Tom Rivers for the Westwood One *Garth Brooks Story* radio show in 1996: "I collect cowboy boots, and I went over there one day and got to talking with him and her. He was saying, 'Yeah I'm trying to get something going. I'm from Oklahoma. I'm a singer-songwriter.' I said, 'Well, I am too,' and I ended up buying a pair of cowboy boots from him. He gave me his business card, and I still have it today.

"I thought that was pretty neat, and a few months later I'm driving down the road and hear him on the radio. Now he's one of the biggest things that ever happened to country music. I guess I can say I met him, you know, back when."

It didn't take long when first searching for live, paying gigs, for Santa Fe to discover that Nashville did not operate like other cities. Bar gigs were plentiful, especially in the honky-tonks on Lower Broadway like Tootsies and Robert's Western Wear, but the bands played only for tips. Plus, the club owners frowned on acts performing original material. Most Nashville bands, they realized, were essentially live jukeboxes cranking out classic Merle Haggard and George Jones hits as they played stamina-sapping, four-hour sets.

The alternative was to perform at songwriter clubs, which were mostly no use for loud live bands like Santa Fe. Their only real option was to play an appropriate showcase gig, at a venue suited to a band, and to get as many industry contacts to the show as humanly possible. They played a showcase at the Sutler, a run-down bar on Franklin Road, but when their original songs failed to generate any real reaction, they reverted to covers just to survive the gig.

Following the showcase, it proved too much to bear for most, and the band voted not to carry on. "It was fun for the first month, living with your dreams," Brooks told Marje McGraw for a December 1, 1992, *Saturday Evening Post* article, "but once again reality rang the doorbell. It just fell apart right in front of our eyes." Most of the band members returned to Oklahoma, leaving Garth and Sandy with the house that they could no longer afford, but with their still-intact dreams of success.

If the band route wasn't going to work out for Brooks, he decided, he'd go it alone. Fortunately, Sandy was prepared to tough it out with him. She worked while Brooks devoted himself to meeting the right people and writing songs, whether alone or with as many of Nashville's established names as he could persuade to work with him.

Bob Doyle was not a typical Nashville artist manager. Outwardly he looked more like a financial adviser or a university professor, perhaps. No shades, no cowboy boots, no Western affectation or ostentation in any form—there was nothing on the surface to suggest that this neatly business-suited gent would guide a young, hopeful country singer to become a game-changing, record-obliterating, world superstar. But Nashville was in transition, and young, well-educated business guys, like Doyle, Kerry O'Neil, and Rusty Jones—who later became Brooks's long-term associates—were the new face of Nashville's recording and publishing industries.

Brooks and Sandy had to relocate after Santa Fe dissolved, and they moved into a house owned by Stephanie Brown. Like Bob Childers, who felt the urge to connect the ebullient Brooks with his best contact, Stephanie Brown figured she had the perfect industry contact for her songwriter protégé.

Bob Doyle was director of membership relations at the ASCAP Nashville office and had a solid Nashville reputation as a straight shooter. Brown trusted his opinion and knew that he had a good ear for a song. She played Doyle a very rough demo of a song called "Much Too Young (to Feel This Damn Old)," a well-crafted song that Brooks had written with his Stillwater pal Randy Taylor.

In October 2014, Taylor told *American Songwriter*'s Rick Moore that his key contribution had been suggesting that they change the protagonist from a singer to a rodeo cowboy. "Garth and I had done some writing together, and one night he sat down and played "Much Too Young" for

RIGHT: Tootsie's Orchid Lounge on Nashville's Broadway. It has a back door that opens onto the Ryman Auditorium's stage door. It was Hank Williams's favorite bar, and a place that Garth would have loved for Santa Fe to play.

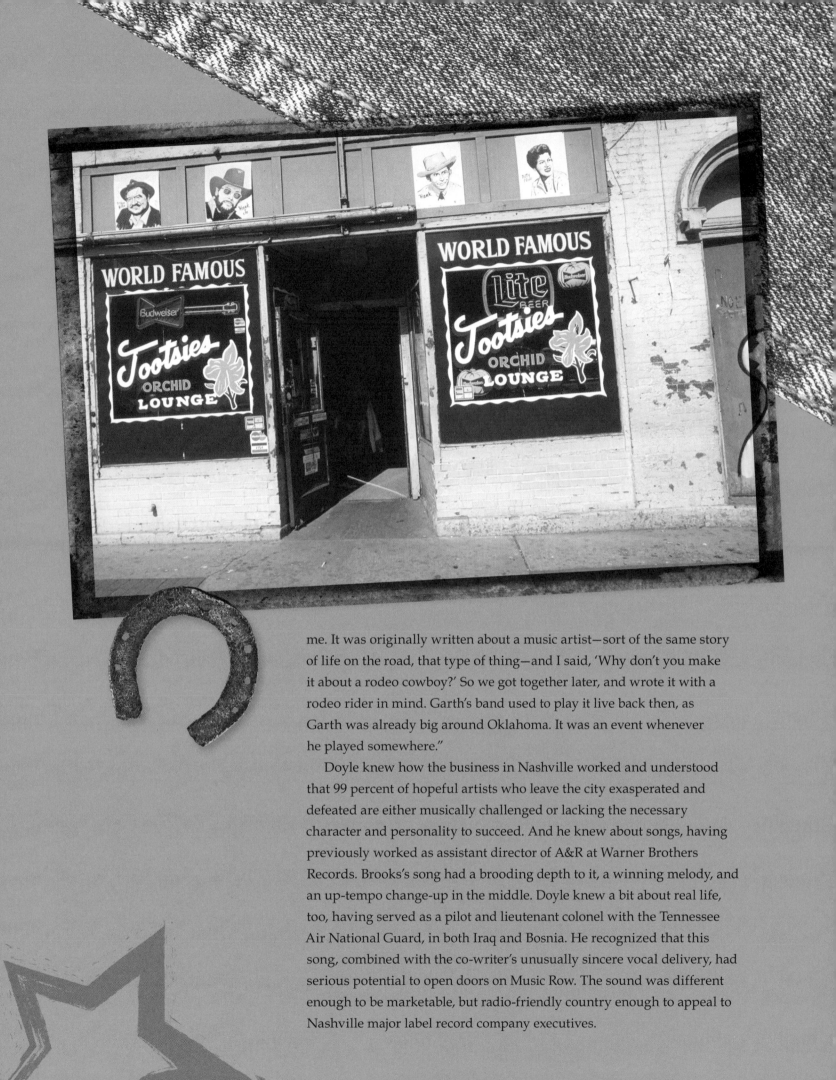

me. It was originally written about a music artist—sort of the same story of life on the road, that type of thing—and I said, 'Why don't you make it about a rodeo cowboy?' So we got together later, and wrote it with a rodeo rider in mind. Garth's band used to play it live back then, as Garth was already big around Oklahoma. It was an event whenever he played somewhere."

Doyle knew how the business in Nashville worked and understood that 99 percent of hopeful artists who leave the city exasperated and defeated are either musically challenged or lacking the necessary character and personality to succeed. And he knew about songs, having previously worked as assistant director of A&R at Warner Brothers Records. Brooks's song had a brooding depth to it, a winning melody, and an up-tempo change-up in the middle. Doyle knew a bit about real life, too, having served as a pilot and lieutenant colonel with the Tennessee Air National Guard, in both Iraq and Bosnia. He recognized that this song, combined with the co-writer's unusually sincere vocal delivery, had serious potential to open doors on Music Row. The sound was different enough to be marketable, but radio-friendly country enough to appeal to Nashville major label record company executives.

JAMES TAYLOR

ntrospective, angst-ridden, sensitive, and poetic, James Taylor (b. March 12, 1948), was the epitome of the singer-songwriter movement that surfaced in America at the beginning of the 1970s. The fact that he was "discovered" by the Beatles added to his kudos. His lifelong struggle with depression and battle against drugs have given his music an intimacy and depth of meaning that his fans cherish, finding his willingness to address subject matter that isn't pure romance or cliché brave and touching. Garth Brooks first came across Taylor in 1972, at just ten years old, when Brooks's older brother Mike brought home Taylor's third album, *Mud Slide Slim and the Blue Horizon* (1971). By the time that track number one ("Love Has Brought Me Around") was done playing, Garth was hooked.

America had taken to Taylor in 1970, when the single version of "Fire and Rain" from his sophomore release, *Sweet Baby James,* made #3 on the pop charts. But the really big hit came in 1971, with his version of his friend Carole King's "You've Got a Friend." It made the #1 spot on the pop charts around the world, and in the process earned the handsome, long-haired Taylor armies of mostly female fans who remained remarkably dedicated to him from then on.

Perhaps Taylor's appeal to the female sex was something that the young Brooks realized and appreciated. Chatting to the audience for his comeback solo shows in Las Vegas in 2009, Garth introduced a segment of songs written and/or originally performed by James Taylor with a story about meeting his hero. "How much did James influence my life?" he asked rhetorically, answering himself after half a beat. "We named our first child after James!"

He continued to relate the story of how they once appeared on the same music television show. "VH1

does a show called *VH1 Honors,*" he explained, "and they pair artists with his or her hero. James Taylor didn't get paired with his hero. I did." Before the taping of that show, Brooks said, Taylor requested to rehearse in Brooks's dressing room. Brooks was starstruck. "I don't think I'm gay, but this guy was beautiful," he joked.

Originally from Boston, Taylor and his family moved to Chapel Hill, North Carolina, when his father took a teaching position at the University of North Carolina School of Medicine. Inspired by the pop and folk boom of the early 1960s, James Taylor picked up the guitar and played folk and blues sets in local coffee houses with longtime pal Danny Kortchmar. Before he could start at college, Taylor fell into a dark and deep depression, and in 1965 he committed himself to a hospital in Massachusetts.

After nine months, during a brief period of positivity and recovery, Taylor moved to New York to further his musical ambitions, but once again his fragile mental state affected him adversely. Taylor began using heroin, and that, combined with more bouts of depression, saw him returning home to North Carolina for more treatment. A change of pace and scenery seemed like a good idea and, in 1967, Taylor moved to London, epicenter of the swinging sixties pop scene.

Taylor recorded some tunes on a basic two-track recorder in Soho, London, and somehow got the tape to Peter Asher, who was about to be named A&R person for Apple Records, the Beatles' wholly-owned record company. Asher loved the sound and took the songs to Paul McCartney and George Harrison. They agreed to Taylor becoming Apple Records' first signing.

His self-titled debut LP failed to set the charts alight in 1969, but it did feature the haunting classic "Carolina in My Mind." With more promotion the album might

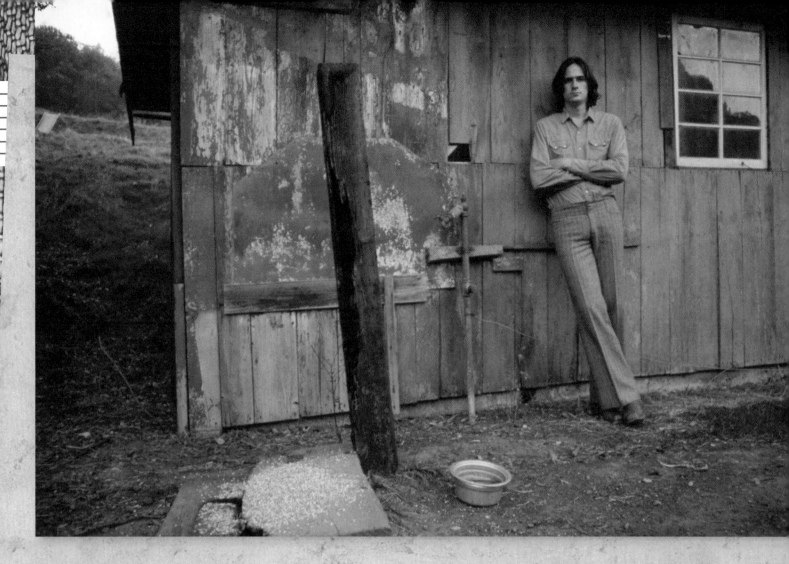

have succeeded, but Taylor was sick again. His heroin addiction had become severe, and he returned home to the United States, and had another stay at a mental facility to help improve his health.

Although his debut album hadn't sold well, Asher negotiated a new deal for him with Warner Brothers. For his first release for the label he teamed up with his old guitarist friend Kortchmar, who offered an important sense of stability and familiarity to Taylor's life and working practices. Leland Sklar played bass, Russ Kunkel drums, and, importantly, Carole King played piano for the recordings. *Sweet Baby James* appeared in early 1970, and set the bar high for all singer-songwriter albums of that decade. It featured that first hit single, "Fire and Rain," plus "Sunny Skies," "Country Road," and, of course, "Sweet Baby James." For a brief moment in 1970, it looked as if Taylor might become a star of the big screen as well as the music business, when he starred alongside (Beach Boy) Dennis Wilson and Warren Oates in a cult movie titled *Two-Lane Blacktop*. Despite good reviews from the underground press, the movie was a box-office flop, but it soon

James Taylor, photographed by Henry Diltz for the cover of *Sweet Baby James*, 1970.

became a staple of late-night cinemas everywhere.

The relationship with Carole King that began in 1970 continued with *Mud Slide Slim* and "You've Got a Friend." Also appearing on the album was Joni Mitchell, and subsequent Taylor albums would feature some of America's finest female singer-songwriters, including his then-wife, Carly Simon (they married in 1972), and Linda Ronstadt, Linda McCartney (plus husband Paul), and Bonnie Raitt. There was always a host of notable musicians on the personnel listing of Taylor albums. Everyone loves James Taylor it seems, and even when the hit singles dried up following "Her Town Too," a duet with J. D. Souther in 1981, that made #11 on the pop charts, there were albums that always sold phenomenally well—in 2008, his album of cover versions titled simply *Covers* (which included his version of George Jones's "Why Baby Why") made #4 on the national album chart. Naturally, his songs peppered Garth's Las Vegas residency from 2009 to 2012.

Once Bob Doyle met Brooks in person and witnessed that remarkable mix of intensity, sincerity, and humility that would drive him to the very top of the entertainment business, he offered to find Brooks a publishing deal. When Doyle discovered that few others in Nashville shared his vision, the former Air Force pilot made a leap of faith. If he couldn't convince a publishing company to sign Brooks, he'd start his own. Doyle took out a second mortgage on his home and put his future in the hands of a new artist from Oklahoma, an artist who had quit the game once before when the going got tough.

Ironically it was the fact that it was Doyle, a typically conservative and ultra-cautious executive, who was risking so much on a new face, that allowed Garth Brooks to be taken seriously within the songwriting community. Doyle would not back a no-hoper, nor would he give up the security of a senior ASCAP position if he didn't think he'd found gold.

Doyle was calm and efficient and knew what Nashville wanted in a new artist. What he lacked was some marketing and PR pizzazz to spread the word about Garth. The perfect job, he thought, for an outgoing publicist with marketing savvy from New York named Pam Lewis.

Lewis was well educated, a graduate of Wells College with a BA in economics/marketing, and she'd done post-grad work at New York's Fordham University. Following that she was lured into showbiz via the excitement being stirred by what would become a major cultural force in pop culture, MTV.

Lewis was part of the revolutionary cable channel's initial publicity team. When she moved into the record business it was with RCA, who wanted her street-smart PR savvy in Nashville, working with acts like Dolly Parton, Kenny Rogers, the Judds, and Alabama. When RCA made departmental changes Lewis was left out in the cold, a move that led to her forming her own public relations company, PLA Media, where she picked up maverick, rebellious clients like Steve Earle and Richard Dobson.

Lewis was tough, she thought outside the box, and possessed the kind of creativity allied with tenacity that Bob Doyle respected—and needed. He asked to bring her in to work with his new discovery from Oklahoma. Lewis was excited by the challenge. Being part of a start-up business appealed to her sense of adventure and nonconformity. Brooks, an obviously driven and talented young artist with little baggage attached, was appealing after the drama she was used to with her more esoteric singer-songwriter clients. He didn't drink, his mother had been a professional singer, and he was a former college athlete, a good talker, and a good listener. The press releases wrote themselves, and the media would embrace him. Lewis was absolutely confident of Brooks's appeal. All they had to do was convince everyone else.

> "Garth Brooks is an organization of people ... Believe me, if there were hands on the wheel, they weren't mine."
>
> GARTH BROOKS

When Doyle, as Brooks's song publisher, put Garth on a modest $300 a week draw (an advance against royalties), he was able to spend much more time writing songs, co-writing with others and taking as many meetings as Doyle and Lewis could arrange. While Doyle and Lewis planned a promotional campaign, went through demo tapes, and set up photo shoots, Brooks attended writers' nights, as many as he could find. While country music wasn't enjoying the same kind of economic boom that hit Nashville in the 1990s, the late '80s saw an influx of songwriters moving in on the heels of the 1986 breakthrough albums of writer-artists like Lyle Lovett, Steve Earle, and Dwight Yoakam. New arrivals simply picked up a copy of the weekly entertainment paper, the *Nashville Scene*, and pored though its club listings section for songwriter nights. There were nights at the Broken Spoke, a hotel bar in a seedy part of East Nashville; in the lounge of the Holiday Inn on West End Ave; downtown at the Windows on the Cumberland Room close to the river; at the

Sutler and Douglas Corner, both on the road out of Nashville headed to Franklin, where the big stars like Tammy Wynette and George Jones lived. Some nights five or six established writers would take turns to sing and play their material; other nights were open mic affairs where anyone could put their name on a piece of paper and wait their turn to sing their songs.

Songwriter nights were essential for those looking for their break, for several reasons. It was a chance to hear new material (and every artist needs the best songs), it was an opportunity to be seen by someone significant in the business, and, perhaps most usefully, it was an opportunity to meet other songwriters of different levels of ability and career progression.

One of the first fellow songwriters Brooks met was Bryan Kennedy, at the Bluebird Café, in the summer of 1987. (To prove the point about the benefit of meeting other songwriters, Kennedy has written several songs with Brooks over the years, including "Rodeo and Juliet" on Brooks's 2014 album, *Man Against Machine*.) Kennedy told the story of his first Brooks encounter to Harry Chapman during an "audience with" session at Belmont University. "Believe it or not, back then nobody wore Wrangler blue jeans, nobody wore roper boots, and nobody wore a Resitol cowboy hat. I had all that on. He had all that on, and we spent the night kind of looking at each other across the room at the Bluebird going, 'Who's that guy?' So he gets up and he sings these songs that just blew me away. Dad [top producer Jerry Kennedy] had sent me there. He was like, 'go find me some songs.' I remember going up to a couple of label people, and saying, 'You're gonna sign that guy right?' And they went 'who?' It just blew me away."

Brooks, like everyone else performing at the Bluebird Café, had auditioned to get that Sunday spot where Kennedy first saw him. Amy Kurland, Bluebird's founder, told BBC Four for the 2004 *History of Country Music* series, "I remember his audition day very well because he ran in here late, because I still have his application from that day and I remember writing 'Late' across the top of it. He sang a song and the audience went crazy for it. It was one of those magic Bluebird moments, and in years of Sunday night writers nights, we have had very few standing ovations—and that's the first one I remember. In this small room with no band and no trapezes or anything, he really came across."

In 1987, the most prestigious songwriter night in Nashville was at the Bluebird Cafe. Kathy Mattea had performed there regularly in the early 1980s and had been spotted and signed to a recording contract. From that point on, it was the place to be seen.

The Bluebird had originally been opened by Amy Kurland as an upscale restaurant in a pretty bland strip mall in an affluent Nashville suburb of Green Hills. It was a small room with a bar on one side and

table and chairs crammed tightly around a tiny stage area. You can look in through the glass frontage from the outside, but what you can't be aware of is the hushed-tone policy that patrons adhere to. The club developed into the ultimate home for songwriters because the management treats artists with respect. Chatting patrons are asked to be quiet or leave. The songs are to be heard, not talked over.

When Bryan Kennedy told his father all about the new act he'd witnessed at the Bluebird, he discovered that Jerry had already been told about Garth by Bob Doyle. His son's endorsement served to further intrigue him.

Jerry Kennedy was something of a Nashville industry legend. In the mid-1980s he was running his own production company (JK Productions), but his track record before that was impressive, to say the least. A guitar prodigy in his home state of Louisiana, Kennedy got his big break by playing guitar on the *Louisiana Hayride* radio show.

When his music partner and friend Shelby Singleton moved to

Nashville to work at Mercury Records, Kennedy moved, too, and quickly found plenty of session work. He played on country classics like the classic "Harper Valley P.T.A." by Jeannie C. Riley, and Roy Orbison's hit ballad "Oh, Pretty Woman," helped Jerry Lee Lewis convert from rock and roll to country music, and contributed both guitar and Dobro to album sessions by rock and rollers like Dylan (on *Blonde on Blonde*), Elvis, and Ringo Starr. Not content with making a good living as a Nashville cat, Kennedy also wrote songs and worked as a producer (for Roger Miller's early hits) and as a record-company executive, becoming Mercury's vice president of country music in the 1970s.

Jerry Kennedy, with his son's recommendation ringing in his ears, listened to Brooks again and made a career-changing decision. He recorded some new demos of material written or co-written by Brooks.

In order to make more inroads into the Nashville community, Doyle offered Garth as a demo singer to a songwriter he knew, Kent Blazy, who had recently built his own studio and was busy producing demo sessions for publishing companies. Blazy had been in Nashville since 1980, initially as a songwriter, and had scored cuts with Gary Morris, Moe Bandy, and Exile in his first year in town. Then, after the hits dried up he borrowed money to build a studio and record demos for others. Two of the singers he used were Billy Dean and Trisha Yearwood, who belted out potential hits for $10 a song. Blazy met Brooks at the end of 1987, and in February 1988 they began writing songs together. The first song they worked on was an idea Brooks had been throwing at every writer he met.

"The idea was Garth's," Blazy told *Country Weekly* magazine's Bob Paxman in 2001. "He told me that he had run it by about 50 other writers, hoping to find someone to write the song with him, but none of them took any interest in it. They thought the title was too depressing. He kind of knew how the first verse should go, and what we should talk about in that verse. Then we bounced words and ideas back and forth. We started writing the song for our own voices, and that helped us finish it." "It" was, of course, "If Tomorrow Never Comes."

Finding a record deal, however, proved a thankless task, for a while. Every major label in Nashville rejected Doyle and Lewis's protégé, including Jimmy Bowen at MCA, who thought him too pop, while others didn't rate him as a singer. Jim Fogelsong, head honcho at Capitol, liked what he saw but wasn't convinced enough to make any kind of an offer. A demo tape, even a meet-up with Brooks in person was not enough to convince Nashville's so-called artist experts of the Oklahoma singer's talent, or even his potential talent.

But for a few, like Jerry Kennedy, Doyle, and Lewis, it was obvious that it was just a matter of time before significant doors opened for Garth Brooks. Kennedy tipped off an old booking agent friend, Joe Harris at Buddy Lee Attractions, and Brooks, remarkably, scored an agent before he found a label, which was a very unusual situation in the interplay between agents and record companies. There were several small booking agencies involved in country music in the middle part of the 1980s, all fighting to find tour dates and prestigious gigs for their clients. However, Buddy Lee Attractions was far from small. It was possibly the best agency in the business at that point. Joe Harris was working his own roster of acts at Buddy Lee Attractions through the '80s, Joe Stampley, Razzy Bailey, Helen Cornelius, and Mel McDaniel among them. McDaniels's producer, Jerry Kennedy, chose Joe Harris to tip off about the act he believed was the next big thing in country music. Harris called Brooks's management and set up a meeting. Following it, Harris agreed that Brooks was an unusual and a special talent and wanted the company to break its rule of only signing acts with a recording contract, and he talked the co-owner of the company, Tony Conway, into agreeing with him.

Conway later recalled the meeting in an interview with Gary James of Classicbands.com: "The day that I met Garth he came up to our office. He had an appointment with one of our agents, Joe Harris. He had actually walked in off the street and dropped a work tape off and Joe listened to it. He was in Joe's office with an acoustic guitar, demoing some stuff he'd written, and I was walking down the hall and I heard this powerful voice coming out of the office. I walked in and pretty soon there were ten people that had been in there. It was just riveting. He had a very unique way and style about him that I hadn't really seen in a long time. It was almost like a magnetic star power type of thing. So, we said 'you're signed today. You want you to deal with us, we'll do it!' And we signed him that day." Harris then went to work utilizing every contact in his well-thumbed phone book to get Brooks live work.

Ironically, one of the gigs Harris came up with was back in Stillwater, as a stand-in for Pake McEntire (Reba's brother), who'd been double-booked. Ray Bingham, the show's producer, told *Tulsa World* in 1997, "I called Joe Harris down at Buddy Lee Attractions in Nashville and he said, 'Hell, Garth'd be perfect for that, being as how it's in Stillwater, where he went to school.'" The gig was a success, and Brooks, showing that rare command of social skills that would enamor him to so many over the early part of his career, made sure the promoter knew he appreciated the opportunity. "Right after that," said Bingham, "Garth sent me a letter, thanking me for booking him on his first professional job."

Garth was making progress, but was still looking for that all–so-important and very prestigious major label record deal. In the spring of 1988 it seemed as if everyone at major record labels in Nashville had passed. But on May 11 someone who hadn't yet heard him happened upon a performance by Garth by accident. That evening Lynn Shults, VP of A&R at Capitol Records, was at the Bluebird Cafe to see one of Nashville's most promising songwriters of the day, Ralph Murphy. He

BELOW: Some of the people who helped shape Gath's career from the beginning: L-R manager Bob Doyle, producer Allen Reynolds, songwriter Pat Alger, Garth, songwriters Jenny Yates and Kent Blazy.

hadn't heard that Murphy had canceled his appearance, though, and instead there was a new young performer booked to replace him—which was no easy task, given that Murphy had a growing reputation of note, and the Bluebird crowd was famous for not taking kindly to poor, nervous performers.

"It totally came out of the blue for me," Brooks remembered to *Billboard*'s Chick Dauphin in 2014. "Ralph Murphy was supposed to play at the Bluebird, and he was sick. They asked if I would go on in his place, but they were there to see him. That's what happened to me. I know it's about luck, but when they hand you the ball, that's when you have to try to do the best that you can."

Shults was an experienced music man who had worked at Nashville

institutions like the Acuff-Rose music publishing company, Starday/King Records, RCA Records, and United Artists Records. He had rubbed shoulders with numerous country music heavyweights, from Kenny Rogers to Crystal Gayle and Tanya Tucker. Shults told Ed Morris of *Billboard*, "Being on the road with a lot of great artists you get this frame of reference for what is exceptional. And that night, Garth was exceptional."

He also told Ed Morris (as reported on CMT.com in June 2003) that there was no comparison between the Garth Brooks who played some songs in the Capitol Records office and the guy who connected so magnificently with every person in the room at the Bluebird Café. "What went through my mind was that I had just seen somebody who was as good as—if not better than—anyone I had ever seen. . . . Immediately after he finished, I went over to Bob Doyle, who was standing by the bar, and I said, 'You guys got a deal, and as far as I'm concerned, it's an album deal.'"

Garth Brooks signed his contract with Capitol Records on June 17.

5

Friends in Low Places

As 1988 progressed, Team Brooks was almost complete. There was Bob Doyle, using his network of connections and his deep understanding of the songwriting business. Joe Harris was scheduling live dates. Pam Lewis was applying her always creative and inventive marketing tactics. And of course Garth was utilizing his particular brand of near-obsessive drive and magnetism.

All that remained was to find the right person to add the shine to the music—which is where record producer Allen Reynolds came in. Demo producer and early Garth champion Jerry Kennedy opted out of the deal with Capitol, leaving an opening for a different record producer to work with the singer. Team Brooks understood that Garth's music needed to be honed in the studio by someone who was steeped in tradition but also open minded to other styles and genres and who, like Brooks, believed in the power of a song.

"Songs are what drive this whole thing along," Brooks told me in 1988. "Nashville is a songwriting town, and there are some incredible writers here, and my job is to write songs that are good enough to compete with these guys and to find the best songs in town and then put it all together."

Allen Reynolds (b. August 18, 1938), was a songwriter, a song hunter and collector, and a song publisher, as well as being an experienced producer with a reputation for putting the artist first. He was no prima donna Phil Spector–style producer, but rather a man who put himself in the background so as to put the spotlight on the song and the singer.

Reynolds started out as an English major at Rhodes College in Memphis in the late 1950s, but two friendships sent him in a musical rather than literary direction. Classmate Dickey Lee (who would later write the country classic "She Thinks I Still Care") liked to write songs, and Reynolds recognized that he, too, also had an aptitude for crafting a three-minute musical wonder. Both students became friends with a young engineer named Jack "Cowboy" Clement (1931–2013), who worked at Sun Records, which was famous for having launched the careers of Elvis Presley, Jerry Lee Lewis, and Johnny Cash, to name a few (Cowboy Jack wrote "Ballad of a Teenage Queen" for Cash in 1957). When Cowboy Jack left Memphis for Texas in 1961, to start his own studio, Reynolds and Dickey Lee went with him.

Not long after, Lee and Reynolds made their mark as songwriters when Dickey Lee made the Top 20 of the US pop chart with their "I Saw Linda Yesterday" single for Smash Records, a division of Mercury Records, which would help turn Jerry Lee Lewis into a country singer.

After the Beatles invaded America in 1964, Reynolds and Lee headed back to Memphis and set up their own publishing and production company. In 1965 they gave the Vogues a Top 5 pop hit with Reynolds's

"Five O'clock World," released on the Pittsburgh-based Co & Ce label (where Lou Christie began his career).

Reynolds ended the swinging sixties by moving to Nashville to work for Jack Clements at his JMI Records as a producer and studio manager. Reynolds stayed in Nashville, and he eventually bought Jack's Tracks recording studio from Clement. There, over a twenty-year period, he produced a number of top acts, including Don Williams, Crystal Gayle, Kathy Mattea, and Emmylou Harris. "The interesting thing about Allen Reynolds," Don Williams told me in Nashville in 1991, "is that he likes to try different things." Williams recorded for JMI Records in the early 1970s alongside the coolest of the cool Music City musicians, Kenny Malone, Lloyd Green, and Chuck Cochran. "With Allen we kept it simple to let the song shine and be the focus on the record." Williams continued,

"I guess he learned from Cowboy that you can try different sounds and style so long as the song is the main thing. Sounds obvious, but you'd be surprised how many Nashville producers don't think that way at all."

Several producer names had been thrown around once Brooks had his Capitol contract, but Lynn Shults was a fan of Allen Reynolds, as well as of Bob Doyle. Pam Lewis felt that Reynolds's all-around music savvy as well as his "folk meets country and rock-and-roll" background would be the right fit for her new act.

Happily, once the artist and potential producer met, it was clear to all and sundry that Team Brooks had found its musical director. If Shults, Doyle, and Lewis played a three-headed version of the Beatles' manager and discoverer Brian Epstein, then Garth Brooks now had his very own George Martin. Brooks, being young and naïve but extremely driven, was perfectly complemented by the mild-mannered veteran songman, who had a wealth of multi-genre experience. Reynolds would become the linchpin for the phenomenal sales success that was about to shake Nashville to its core.

> # "You can either sit on your ass and condemn other people for trying things, or you can go out and try and do all the stuff you possibly can."
>
> ## GARTH BROOKS

"You have to trust your producer, and he has to trust you. Allen Reynolds and I have that kind of relationship," Garth told me at his management offices in January 1994. "Once I sat down and talked with Allen I knew he was the right guy."

As for the sound, Brooks knew exactly what he wanted to accomplish. As he explained to the *Chicago Tribune*'s Jack Hurst in an interview in April 1989. "I wanted a George Jones hard-country feel with a Dan Fogelberg or James Taylor orientation toward lyrics. With every song, you've got a chance to get on a soapbox and tell a nation something, and you might as well tell them something that needs to be said. . . . If the songs were funny, I wanted them to be clever, and if they were serious I wanted them to be real deep, to reach in there and try to grab you by the heart."

There was a remarkable resurgence in songwriting that year in Nashville. Veteran songwriter and hero to all newcomers Harlan Howard hosted a parking lot party for his birthday every year. That night in September 1988, the place was teeming with hungry young writers, inspired by the new wave of country forcing itself onto country radio and the new breed of songwriters and artists, from songwriting performer and winner of the 1988 CMA New Male Vocalist Award Rodney Crowell and New Female Vocalist Award Winner Suzy Bogguss, to those songwriters who preferred to stay away from the microphone, like Don Schlitz and Paul Overstreet.

Brooks was part of that community. He attended songwriter nights, listened to songs, and picked up demo cassettes wherever he could. As he drove the fifteen or twenty minutes home to Hendersonville from the Bluebird Café or the Sutler or Douglas Corner, or whatever songwriter showcase or open mic night he'd picked for that evening, he could check out the songs on his car tape player, looking for a hit, searching for writers he could relate to. And Brooks, more than most, understood the songwriting and songwriter dynamic. He was one of them, and if he had a deal then he'd use some of their songs on his project.

Brooks was a good writer. He could have filled his debut album with self-written material (at the time George Jones had been considering recording "If Tomorrow Never Comes," for instance), but that would have set him apart from a community of writers that was coming up with some startling material in Nashville in that period.

In October 2012, Allen Reynolds was interviewed on stage for the Country Music Hall of Fame's "Poets and Prophets" series of events, and he spoke glowingly about how Garth Brooks instinctively understood the power of the right song when they were working on his debut album. "He impressed me thoroughly. We had cut the songs and decided [that] one of them we didn't want to use, and needed to cut a tenth song to finish the album. It was the first album and we had a lot of songs on hand. He had been writing for a good while when we met, and he'd also been gathering songs. But his name was already on five songs and that was his self-imposed limit. We were stuck for a few weeks until I presented him with a song that Jack Clement wrote that I had always loved, and he liked it ["I Know One," a #1 hit for Jim Reeves in 1960].

"That was the way he was. He said, 'I'd like to hope that I can be a good

RIGHT: In 1988, the year that Garth signed his recording contract, Texan singer-songwriter Rodney Crowell (right) was awarded the New Male Vocalist of the Year Award by the Academy of Country Music. Suzy Bogguss (left) won the New Female Vocalist of the Year Award. Garth would win the New Male Vocalist of the Year Award two years later.

ABOVE: Garth loved nothing better than to get on stage with his heroes—Charlie Daniels (center) and Chris LeDoux.

enough writer to write some of my material, but I don't want to send the message to the songwriters that I'm gonna write them all, 'cos I need them and I need their songs.' He meant songs that he did not write that are so important to his career, like "Friends in Low Places." Big records that if he had been closed to, and not willing to hear, he'd never have had, and his career would be shrunken."

So they went to work in Jack's Tracks at 1308 16th Avenue South on Music Row. Reynolds took great care with every number, making sure the songs worked for Brooks and fit the overall sound of the project. This was very much an album to be listened to in its entirety, not just as a

collection of cool new songs. The album was released in April 1989, and simply titled *Garth Brooks*. While the record was initially overshadowed by Clint Black's truly excellent *Killin' Time* album, both in the music press and in terms of sales, Brooks's debut was nevertheless well reviewed. Jack Hurst of the *Chicago Tribune* enthused that it was "an excellent LP by a newcomer whose talent should enable him to hang around a long time. Offering a fine voice with a strong bent toward the ultra-country side of the spectrum, Brooks' music is more than a little western, as well."

Indeed, and the first single, that old tune Brooks had written with Randy Taylor back in Oklahoma, "Much Too Young (to Feel This Damn Old)" made the country music Top 10. Not only was it a solidly traditional country song with a clever tempo change, but Brooks received much industry attention for his mention of rodeo cult hero and singer-songwriter Chris LeDoux in the lyrics.

Hurst continued: "His songs, five of which he wrote or co-wrote, combine humor, overpowering emotion and sometimes-steamy sexiness. There's a wide range of fine stuff here, but two of the sleepers may be his funny ode to small town somnolence, "Nobody Gets off in This Town" and his sensitive remake of a Jim Reeves classic, "I Know One." This is star-quality stuff."

The next single, the song that convinced Capitol Records to sign him, was Brooks's emotive "If Tomorrow Never Comes," released in July 1989. It eventually made it to the top of the country chart on December 9, that year. The album ultimately topped out at #2 on the US country album chart and climbed into the Top 20 of the *Billboard* 200 pop album chart. Its crossover success owed a great deal to the fourth single, the bittersweet "The Dance," which remains perhaps Brooks's best-loved song.

"The Dance" is what industry insiders call a "career song." It announced the arrival of an artist who possessed that rare ability to totally absorb himself in another writer's material, and make the song his own. Brooks first heard Tony Arata, who had only been pursuing music in Nashville for a couple of years himself, at the Bluebird singing this unusual but powerful country song. Like Brooks's best material it was emotive and soulful, tinged with just the right amount of sentimental sadness for the bittersweet element to be effective rather than slushy.

In an interview with QuestionForLiving.com on September 20, 2011, Arata recalled how the song came about. "I went to see a movie called *Peggy Sue Got Married* with Kathleen Turner and Nick Cage. Long story short, she goes back in time but with all the knowledge that she had learned in her later years. Nick Cage proposes to her and this time she knows how horrible it all turned out, so she tells him 'No.' After doing so she looks at the locket around her neck and the pictures of her children are not there. The scene hit me so hard—if she doesn't marry him, she doesn't get her kids. We don't get to pick and choose our memories. I went

home and wrote the words that you know in about 30 minutes. Because then I knew what the song was supposed to be about."

"The Dance" had something significant in common with the equally sentimental and emotive "If Tomorrow Never Comes." Both songs told very dramatic stories, and as the Brooks team understood, a visual interpretation could make or break a song. Pop and rock music had been revolutionized by the music video after MTV's launch in the early 1980s. Country music was a little further behind that, but country videos were beginning to make an impact on their market. CMT, Country Music Television, was Nashville's answer to MTV. It had developed out of a

ABOVE: Chris LeDoux in action on stage with his band; one of Garth's greatest inspirations when developing his stagecraft.

setup called CMTV in Hendersonville in 1983, and it rocked along nicely until in 1991, it was picked up by a larger company, Gaylord, who pushed it heavily alongside their other music channel, the Nashville Network, or TNN, ensuring that it would be seen on a plethora of cable channels.

In 1989, both the traditionally inclined TNN and the less conventional CMT played as many music videos as they could that were suitable for their audience. Cable and satellite reach was growing across the United States, especially in rural areas, where many residents had no choice but to install a satellite dish if they wanted to get a decent and watchable picture on their televisions.

Just as new pop and rock acts had realized that video was a crucial marketing and artistic tool in the representation of the song's meaning and its mass exposure, some country acts similarly recognized the potential of the new medium. Brooks wasn't especially comfortable seeing himself up close on screen or acting out a drama at first, though. "I could do without the acting part, but you know, the whole video process is interesting and brings a new dimension to a song, so it's pretty neat in that way," he told me at a breakfast at Shoney's Diner on Demonbreun Street in Nashville in June 1989.

> "To me Garth, he's kind of like my guardian angel. It's like every time I need some help, he's there"
>
> CHRIS LEDOUX

Pam Lewis had been involved with MTV in its early pioneer days, and she knew absolutely that as a marketing tool, the TNN and CMT networks would play major roles in promoting her and Doyle's new act. "Obviously video was the future," Lewis told me at her 16th Avenue South office in 1999. "Not everyone in Nashville figured that out very quickly, but we just knew how important the video itself and the networks' rotation of particular songs would be. I knew then that CMT would grow and grow, maybe not as much or as fast as it did, but it was gonna be a factor, for sure."

When Garth Brooks name checked Chris LeDoux on his debut single, "Much Too Young (to Feel This Damn Old)" in 1989, all but the initiated knew who he was singing about. Although LeDoux (October 2, 1948–March 9. 2005), had been making and selling records since the beginning of the decade, they'd mostly been released by himself and on cassette only. Following that name check, though, he began releasing records on the same label as Garth, Capitol, who'd only been clued in to him following their new star's endorsement. On close inspection of LeDoux's singing and performing style, it was easy to see why Brooks was such a massive fan of the rodeo star turned musical performer.

LeDoux, who died from liver cancer age 57, was that increasingly rare thing in the late twentieth century, a genuine singing cowboy. He joined the rodeo circuit as a teenager before turning pro in 1968. He qualified for the prestigious National Finals Rodeo five times, and peaked in 1976, when he won the bareback world title. He retired in 1980, carrying a medical record filled with the usual rodeo rider's injuries, but with an unusual rodeo rider's second career to take up. During his rodeo career, LeDoux had played guitar and sang cowboy standards as well as wrote songs that documented the rodeo lifestyle, performing at rodeos and country fairs—sometimes riding a mechanical bull as his band played on. Before hitting the big time in the '90s, LeDoux released more than twenty albums on his own label.

Blessed with an entrepreneur spirit, he had started his own label with his father, Al, suitably called American Cowboy Records. LeDoux packaged his songs and released them as cassettes, partly because they were most easily and cost-effectively produced and manufactured by his Al on tape duplicating machines in LeDoux's parents' home in Mount Juliet, near Nashville, and also because his fans spent a great deal of time in their cars and trucks, where cassette players were standard. Over the years LeDoux reckoned that he'd sold more than $14 million worth of cassettes.

After retiring from the rodeo circuit, LeDoux and his family settled on a ranch in Kaycee, Wyoming, where he devoted more time to his music career and started playing stage shows farther afield and separate from the rodeo circuit honky-tonks and bars. LeDoux, like Brooks would later do, fused pure Western cowboy material with a rock-and-roll stage show. "I've been banging this triangle between western, country and rock 'n' roll my whole life," he wrote for a record label biography in the 1990s. As his reputation grew, so too did the gigs—in terms of venue capacity and stage theatrics. As well as riding the mechanical bull, LeDoux did plenty of running and jumping off things (including the stage itself), and where possible he began setting off fireworks on stage.

As Garth Brooks said to the *Tennessean* newspaper in 1997, "anyone who has seen Chris LeDoux knows where I get my approach to live performance." While LeDoux's cult rodeo following grew large enough for him to be courted by several record companies in the 1980s, he always refused their offers. Until, that is, he became a national figure thanks to Garth's rapid rise to stardom. Brooks urged Capitol to sign his cowboy hero, and they did as he suggested, although they assigned LeDoux's releases to an imprint called Liberty Records so as not to put their two cowboy hat–toting singing stars in direct competition.

He recorded his debut album, *Western Underground*, in 1991, but it took a while to take off. The follow-up,

Garth tips his hat after playing a song in honor of Chris LeDoux in Times Square in New York, 2005.

Watcha Gonna Do About a Cowboy (1992), fared much better, selling a million copies and making *Billboard*'s Top 10. The title track, which featured backing vocals from Brooks, became LeDoux's debut on *Billboard*'s country Top 10, when it reached #7 in 1992. LeDoux's music career was steady after that, releasing a new album every two years throughout the 1990s.

In 2000, he released one of his finest albums, *Cowboy*, which featured new versions of his early cowboy songs recorded with producer Mac McAnally in Muscle Shoals.

That same year, tragically, LeDoux was diagnosed with primary sclerosing cholangitis, a rare and debilitating liver ailment. When he discovered that LeDoux needed a new liver, Garth Brooks offered part of his own but was found to be an unsuitable donor. "They had to take samples (of his liver)," LeDoux told the Associated Press's Tom Radner in June 2001. "I went through that myself, and three days of that's pretty painful. For him to go through that, it's pretty amazing. I

never would in my wildest dreams think of a guy wanting to offer part of himself. He just heard I needed a liver and made up his mind he was going to make the attempt to have part of his." LeDoux did find a donor, though, and had a transplant in October 2000. The operation was a success, and he returned to his career for a few too-short years. Sadly, though, LeDoux was taken ill with cancer of the bile ducts, and he died on March 9, 2005.

Garth Brooks broke his retirement that year to record a special tribute song to his hero, titled "Good Ride Cowboy." Brooks told CMT, "I knew if I ever recorded any kind of tribute to Chris, it would have to be up-tempo, happy…a song like him…not some slow, mournful song. He wasn't like that. Chris was exactly what our heroes are supposed to be. He was a man's man. A good friend."

Brooks may not have especially enjoyed the acting aspect of music video production, but he was good at it. With "The Dance" and "If Tomorrow Never Comes" he had two songs that perfectly lent themselves to a dramatic video storyline, and Brooks's on-screen depiction showed heartfelt sincerity. His appealing presence helped to compensate for any lack of acting ability. He exuded likeability and humbleness in both videos, and that was what sold them to both the country and the pop audience.

Brooks and video director John Lloyd Miller took country music videos into a rock and pop dimension. They created miniature movies that included emotionally manipulative clips of various American icons who had died young, among them world champion bull rider Lane Frost, singer-songwriter Keith Whitley, Martin Luther King Jr., John Wayne, and the crew of the Space Shuttle *Challenger*, who'd perished on launch in 1986. In order to make things clear about his intentions with the video, Brooks said, "I'd never compare myself to the folks in this video, but if for some reason I have to leave this world unexpectedly, I hope they play "The Dance" for me because I mean that's it; 'I could have missed the pain, but I'd have had to miss the dance.'"

Garth Brooks's debut album was released in what proved to be a good year for music of all kinds. Back then record stores flourished and customers had the opportunity to browse countless record bins and racks of the still relatively recent product development in music, the compact disc. The top albums, critically and commercially, that year included Tom Petty and the Heartbreakers' *Full Moon Fever*, N.W.A.'s *Straight Outta Compton*, Bonnie Raitt's *Nick of Time*, the Pixies' *Doolittle*, Janet Jackson's *Rhythm Nation*, Don Henley's *The End of the Innocence*, and Madonna's *Like a Prayer*, to name but a few.

It was also a good year for country music acts who were trying to shake up their genre, too. The top-selling artists in 1989 included Dwight Yoakam, Randy Travis, and Steve Wariner. It also saw the emergence of another new wave of artists break, dubbed the "Class of '89," led by Clint Black, who was slated to be bigger than anyone on the scene (including Garth Brooks). Lorrie Morgan (whose husband, bluegrass artist Keith Whitley, died in May 1989), launched a solo career that year, while several other influential musicians were emerging, including Suzy Bogguss, Earl Thomas Conley, the Desert Rose Band, Mary Chapin Carpenter, Travis Tritt, and Alan Jackson.

But it was Texas-raised Clint Black who ruled the roost. He had been born in New York (February 4, 1962) but grew up in Houston. Always musically gifted, he started playing in bands when he was very young, having been encouraged to do so by his three older brothers. Black preferred music over classes in high school and built himself a decent

BELOW: One of the best emerging new country stars of 1989, Lorrie Morgan.

(part-time) career playing bars and clubs in Houston's numerous clubs after dropping out of high school. "I would just sit and play for the clientele," he told me in a 1991 interview. "I had to know all kinds of material, from George Strait to Simon and Garfunkel. It was a great training ground."

He clicked musically with another songwriter and guitar player named Hayden Nicholas, and they collaborated on several original songs, eventually pitching their work to local record promoter Sammy Alfano in Katy, Texas. Alfano was impressed enough to pass the tape to his industry contact, ZZ Top's manager, Bill Hamm. Hamm scored Black a deal with RCA Records, and with ZZ Top money and power behind him, Black was launched onto the scene with his debut album *Killin' Time*.

Like Brooks, Clint Black was traditional enough to appeal to country music's mainstream fan base but also so fresh and different enough that

LORRIE MORGAN

outsiders to country music took an interest. Black insisted on recording his debut album with his road band (which was kind of unheard of in Nashville at the time; session experts were expected to play on the albums while road guys stuck to playing gigs). The mostly self-penned album broke country music sales records when its first four singles went to #1 on the *Billboard* country chart.

People forget, Pam Lewis told me in a 2015 interview, "that in that first year Garth was up against Clint Black, and Clint was way ahead. He was the superstar to compete with—and we did everything we could to get Garth to that level." And Team Garth had an unusual strategy. Aside from a handful of superstars like Dolly Parton and Kenny Rogers, very few country artists, historically, had any kind of career outside America.

Bob Saporiti, who ran the Warner Nashville's international department in the 1990s, explained the dilemma to me during a conversation in 2011. "See, I'd always say to artists, 'Build yourself another career. While you are getting started in the U.S., make some trips to Europe, be seen and build an audience. That way when things dip in America, as they will for almost everyone, you still have an audience who love you.' Look at Don Williams, Dwight Yoakam. They took time out to play overseas, and they can still sell out tours over there, which they may not be able to do in the U.S., where the country music scene changes so quickly." But that was unusual thinking in Nashville in the 1980s and 1990s.

Not surprisingly though, Pam Lewis agreed implicitly with Saporiti's progressive thinking. From the very beginning, the company Doyle/ Lewis, at the emphatic urging of Pam Lewis, planned an international career for Brooks. "Too often," Lewis explained to me, "country artists don't consider their international careers until they see a dip in their careers in the United States. We didn't want to do that. It was our intention to build Garth's career in the UK. We knew it would be tough and we wouldn't make any money, but we felt it was important to tough it out and establish a presence there." And not only in the UK, as she continued to explain. "To fully realize that you have to let the country you visit pick the single. France and Germany might want a different single, and you really had to let those offices champion it.

"I remember Jerry Crutchfield was at the label, and he felt Garth had to lose the cowboy hat. What you gonna do? That's who he is. So, understanding that the UK was important to our plan for Garth we brought Tony Byworth on to the team." At the time Byworth was Britain's preeminent country music authority. He'd been involved in the business since the 1960s, first as a journalist and reporter then as creative manager for Acuff-Rose Music, before founding the Byworth-Wootton International public relations consultancy in 1983.

The first introduction of Garth Brooks into the UK came at the time that his debut single, "Much Too Young (to Feel This Damn Old)," was

released in March 1989. Byworth had introduced himself to Pam Lewis soon after she moved into Nashville from New York, and he was a longtime friend of Garth's record producer, Allen Reynolds, whom he had first met in London when Reynolds was in town to attend a CBS convention with his artist Crystal Gayle in the early 1970s. So familiarity was already established, and Byworth was hired on a monthly retainer to provide services on behalf of the artist, not only public relations but

LEFT: Despite record company
executives suggesting that he
lose his hat while touring in
the UK, Garth stuck with it.

keeping in contact with EMI Records' London office, which handled
Brooks's label, Capitol.

Byworth returned to the UK from one of his regular trips to Nashville
in the spring of 1989, with two copies of "Much Too Young (to Feel This
Damn Old)." One was intended for EMI in the hope that the UK-based
label might include Garth as one of their artists in that year's Country
Music Association's annual UK marketing campaign. The other was for
the UK's top country music broadcaster, Wally Whyton.

EMI acknowledged the single but had decided upon a couple of
their other acts for the campaign, with the label manager adding that
he "would keep an eye on Garth and see how well he does in the States."
Whyton was delighted with the record and slated it for a play the
following week in his *BBC Country Club* show, but as a huge soccer fan, he
joked to Byworth, he was worried that he might confuse the name and
introduce the artist as a well-known English soccer player at the time,
Garth Crooks. Unfortunately, when the time came for him to introduce
the disc on air, he did exactly that!

Although Garth Brooks wasn't chosen to take part in any CMA
marketing campaign in the country, he did arrive in Britain to undertake
a schedule of press, radio, and television work in November 1990. Three
months later, on February 24, 1991, he made his British live performance
debut with a sell-out performance at London's small Cambridge Theatre.
Within a couple of years he'd be playing vast arenas in the UK, and Tony
Byworth maintained his working relationship with Garth Brooks right
up until the artist's retirement in late 2000. When the CMA's *Close Up*
magazine ran a feature on Byworth (as CMA Member of the Month in
December 2011), Garth Brooks provided the final comment on the PR:
"Tony Byworth is the most upbeat guy I have ever met. He never stops
working, and he believes in the potential of Country Music reaching
around the globe more than anyone I have ever worked with. I love the
guy." The feeling was mutual, of course.

However, following the release of his debut album and first few
singles, Garth's career still required some work in his native land before
he could truly concentrate on becoming an international star.

Amazingly, Garth Brooks made it to #13 on the main U.S. album chart,
beating Clint Black's *Killin' Time* by some distance (it only made #31 on
the same chart) and outstripping George Strait's *Beyond the Blue Neon*,
released in 1989 (which only reached #92).

Team Garth knew that 1990 was going to be hard work for everyone,
but they could almost smell the success that it would inevitably bring
them all. Garth was given the task of writing and planning a sophomore
album release, while singles from his debut made further inroads into the
American music scene.

GARTH BROOKS

(CAPITOL RECORDS)

RELEASED

April 12, 1989

RECORDED

Jack's Tracks Recording Studios,
Nashville

PRODUCER

Allen Reynolds

CHART POSITIONS

#2 *Billboard* Top Country Albums;
#13 *Billboard* 200

SINGLES

"Much Too Young (to Feel This Damn Old)," "If
Tomorrow Never Comes," "Not Counting You,"
"The Dance."

TRACKS

1. Not Counting You (G. Brooks)
2. I've Got a Good Thing Going
   (L. Bastian/S. Mahl/G. Brooks)
3. If Tomorrow Never Comes (K. Blazy/G. Brooks)
4. Everytime That It Rains (C. Stefli/T. England/
   G. Brooks)
5. Alabama Clay (L. Cordle/R. Scaife)
6. Much Too Young (to Feel This Damn Old)
   (R. Taylor/G. Brooks)
7. Cowboy Bill (L. Bastian/E. Berghoff)
8. Nobody Gets off in This Town
   (L. Bastian/D. Blackwell)
9. I Know One (J. Clement)
10. The Dance (T. Arata)

When he was in a position to admit to it, Garth would say that he remembered being scared to death when his debut album was due for release. He thought that it was an "innocent" album, and in many ways he's right, of course, particularly because there is no track on it that people could immediately recognize, no cover of a country standard that put the debutant firmly into an established country music star's shadow and specific niche. That was either a brave or naïve decision at the time—even Dwight Yoakam, one of Garth's trailblazing inspirations, had put Johnny Cash's "Ring of Fire" and Harlan Howard's "Heartaches by the Number" on his 1986 debut, *Guitars, Cadillacs, Etc.* There is, admittedly, a cover of "I Know One," written by Cowboy Jack Clement, who'd inadvertently helped Garth's career by mentoring the young Allen Reynolds (it was his choice for Garth to record "I Know One"). However, Reeves had his hit way back in 1960, long before Garth and most of his audience had been born. That was not a deliberate attempt to appeal to Reeves's audience, seeing as how Garth's version was a very modern take on it. Garth Brooks did not employ the standard Nashville clichés that always grab sales from its mainly conservative audience. While there's only one song authored solely by Garth—the future hit single "Not Counting You"—his name is on four of the ten tracks featured on its original release (the CD was later reissued with an extra track, "Uptown Down Home Good Ol' Boy"), and that is a sign of an artist choosing to do things his way. The album doesn't mark the

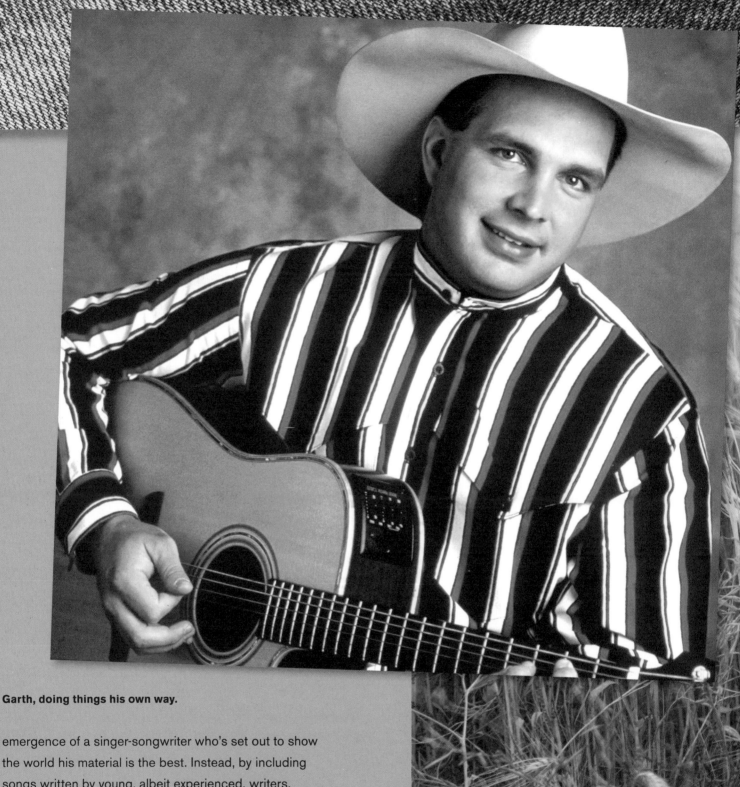

Garth, doing things his own way.

emergence of a singer-songwriter who's set out to show
the world his material is the best. Instead, by including
songs written by young, albeit experienced, writers,
the album shows a performer who not only works with
material written by others, but also actively wants to
work with them. Much was made of the promotional
videos that so brilliantly energized the album's four
singles, but listening to the album when it was released,
you heard the sound of something new to Nashville and
country music; it was the sound of the future coming,
not so slowly, but surely, and with great intention.

6

Superstar!

The great people skills that made Brooks a successful and affable salesman back in the Yukon sports store proved invaluable as his career took off. He won fans and champions everywhere he went in that first year or two in the record business. Pam Lewis was passionate about what she saw as "his sincerity and friendliness." It made her life so much easier to work with an artist that was able to find a rapport with every person he met. Garth exhibited an uncanny ability to remember the names of almost everyone he met in those first few years, and that, allied with his ability to truly focus his attention on the person he was talking to, left everyone he encountered, no matter how briefly, feeling like they were Brooks's best friend.

Lewis had Brooks personally call DJs and radio-station program directors in order to make friends on the airwaves and win support for the upcoming battle to get his material played on all-important radio stations across America—and the rest of the world, too. When Brooks had a chance to meet the nation's radio movers and shakers at 1989's Country Radio Seminar, held at the sprawling Opryland Hotel on the outskirts of Nashville, he grasped the opportunity to seduce almost all of them with his warmth and humble sincerity.

"I can still remember the night when I would have given you a dollar to ten donuts that we weren't going to get signed by a label."

GARTH BROOKS

Each and every radio DJ that I spoke to at Country Radio Seminars from 1989 to 1994, referred to themselves as a personal friend of Garth Brooks. That totaled over one hundred personal friends from all over the world. All of them united in the belief that Garth Brooks and they had a sincere and real friendship.

Garth remembered their names, sometimes recalled their wives' names, and occasionally even their kids' birthdays, too. He took a genuine interest in the people he met, and from the outset refused to allow any kind of a barrier to exist between himself and the audience. It was the same at his live performance shows where he used his Oklahoma-honed technique of talking to, and interacting with, the audience in such a disarming and unaffected manner. The typical "them and us" dynamic that usually separated artist and audience evaporated.

With Garth it wasn't a concert, it was a party, and it wasn't a radio or TV interview, it was just good friends catching up.

It has to be said that Nashville earned a reputation for friendliness and Southern hospitality in 1972, when an annual event titled Fan Fair first occurred. Now renamed CMA Music Fest, in the 1980s and 1990s Fan Fair was held in the same Tennessee State Fairgrounds where it began. From the start, Fan Fair was notable for offering up the amazing experience of seeing some of the music's most prominent and famous singing stars standing in animal pens, albeit pens kitted out with chairs and desks. There they'd stand or sit, next to a stack of photographs or albums ready to be signed for any fans who'd patiently wait their turn to meet, greet, shake hands, and chat with them.

Just a mile or two outside downtown Nashville, it was as friendly and down home as could possibly be and impossibly surreal to fans of other kinds of music, whose star performers would barely look at their fans as they left gigs, hotels, or radio stations.

By the time that Garth began making appearances at Fan Fair, a couple of hundred thousand fans headed for the fairgrounds in sometimes burning tropical-feeling temperatures each June. As well as meeting superstars the attendees also got to watch their musical heroes perform in an outdoor stadium, and eat barbecue roasted by the Chuck Wagon Gang from Texas. At the end of the '80s pretty much anyone who was anyone in country music rented a booth inside the hot and sticky (no air-conditioning back then) livestock barn. It was intimate, friendly, and very "Nashville." Brooks spoke with hundreds of new fans at his first Fan Fair in 1989, and even met some contest winners at the airport, in order to help them with their bags.

Once Garth had secured a recording contract with Capitol Records, his next step was to put together a full-time band and hit the road. Loyalty came high on Brooks's list of priorities as he put together his touring outfit, and one of his first actions after signing on the dotted line for Capitol was to call his old Oklahoma State University roommate, Ty England. "We had this kind of agreement," England explained to me in November 1999, "that the first one of us to get a deal would bring the other in. That's what he did. I just had to decide if I wanted to trade in my stable life with a good steady job that I liked, with benefits and a future, or give it all up for Garth. I thought about it overnight…and then I chose Garth!"

Brooks knew how good a guitarist and fiddle player James Garver was, and wanted him for the band, too. Garver signed on and recommended steel-guitar player Steve McClure, who, as these things go, suggested a drummer—Mike Palmer, an experienced rhythm man who'd spent years playing for Billy "Crash" Craddock. The band was complete.

The band, to be named Stillwater, went to work rehearsing in Brooks's basement. Garth told me in 1989, that the band was more than just a group of back-up musicians. "It's a team, and I love that about it. It's neat to feel the teamwork and their support. When we are on the road we are a unit and we support each other." In country music, artists who are starting out (and occasionally even after they've made a name for themselves) spend much of their lives traveling the country in a tour bus. It's typical for them to play around 250 shows a year supporting their latest album. Of course, touring also provides another income stream aside from record sales and publishing money.

The inclusion of great songs in the set were, naturally, important in the early days, so "If Tomorrow Never Comes" and "The Dance" were fixtures of the Stillwater rehearsal sets. Brooks's intensity and drive added to the creative marketing work from Pam Lewis and Capitol

Records to ensure that Garth's promotional tours and recordings were
the best they could be. And yes, the videos played a vital role in breaking
Brooks onto the world stage. But the one aspect of his truly phenomenal
career that catapulted him (almost literally) to a different level, and
dragged the genre along with him, was his fresh approach to stage work.

"Historically country artists stood still on stage and sang their songs,
maybe tapped a foot or two, and that was pretty much it," country singer
Vince Gill told me in 1984. "That all changed with Garth Brooks and his
spectacular stage show. It was theater. It was a game changer."

Brooks's name check of cowboy star Chris LeDoux on his "Much Too
Young" was no random choice, of course. LeDoux was genuinely an
inspiration, not just in his cowboy persona and literate songwriting,
but mostly because of his frantic, high-energy concert style. The *Denver
Post* in 1999 described LeDoux shows as "a mix of choreographed
mayhem—replete with pyrotechnics and a mechanical bull—and seat-of-
the-pants spontaneity."

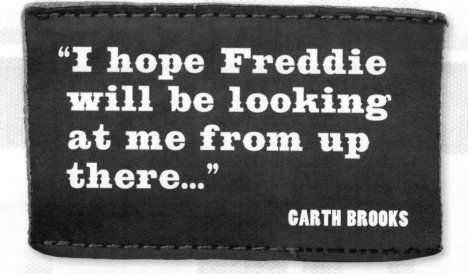

"I hope Freddie
will be looking
at me from up
there..."

GARTH BROOKS

Brooks loved what LeDoux did, seeing in it something close to "KISS
meets cowboys," and he stowed that inspiration away for future reference.
In the meantime, his late '80s show had not reached the excesses and
explosiveness of what would become his trademark performance, but it
was still more energetic, more passionate, and more audience-involved
than anyone else was doing in country music. The singer-songwriter
nights he'd played in Nashville had taught Brooks the valuable art
of communicating with a mature country music audience. His own
attendance at Queen and KISS shows had already impressed on him
the magic that occurs when an artist makes an attempt to connect with
the fans and actually succeeds by using movement, lights, and big, loud,
bright explosions.

"It's not just another show to me. Never has been," Brooks told me in his management offices in Nashville in January 1994. "You gotta think of the guy who has been saving his money to get tickets to see you. The anticipation they have, just like I had when I went to see Freddie Mercury. It's about making every person feel like they matter and that they are part of the show. Because they are!"

The stage shows were designed to be fun, theatrical experiences. It was about much more than faithfully reproducing the album on stage. "We're probably the most flaw-filled band there is," Brooks told the *Boston Globe*'s Steve Morse in 1991. "We like to keep the live show loose. I don't think it's fair to play the songs just the way they are on your compact disc. So we slow our ballads down and pump the fast ones up. I'm just trying to do what I'd like to hear if I were in the audience. And it's only been two and a half years between me standing on stage and me sitting in that audience." But Brooks was never interested in only having a party on stage. His life had been touched by loss while at college, after the deaths of two friends, and the debut album contained enough thoughtful and reflective moments to see that this Brooks was more than just a good-time entertainer. He explained his philosophy to David Huff of *Jam* magazine in February 1990. "I want people to take positive thoughts away with them, little kids especially. I want people to walk away from my show thinking it is hip to be square. It's cool to be old-fashioned. It's alright to go back to having manners and doing what is right."

Perhaps inevitably, with his debut album doing well and live performances earning rave reviews, Brooks began to enjoy life away from Nashville a little too much. Life on the road brings with it much temptation, and while Brooks easily avoided drinking and drugs, readily available sexual favors proved to be another matter. Women were offering themselves to him at every show, and Brooks was enjoying himself, safely cocooned (he believed) by the "code of the road," a variation of "what happens in Vegas, stays in Vegas." Somehow, though, Sandy Brooks discovered her husband's infidelity. She called Garth on the phone and warned him that either he stops or she's leaving. A visibly distraught Garth Brooks, carrying his transparency with the audience to its ultimate conclusion, confessed his guilt the next night to a crowd in Cape Giradeau, Missouri. He broke down during the song he had written while watching Sandy sleep, "If Tomorrow Never Comes."

Brooks learned his lesson and was scared into action by his wife's ultimatum. He explained his feeling to *Playboy*'s Steve Pond. "I was really lost. It's the same old thing, 'I'm working all the time and I'm misunderstood.' It was one of those times that you look back on and say, 'What a crock of ****.' Everything you justified it with is about as thin as water. It was a time that I am not proud of. It was a time that I learned from, so I will not go through it again."

The first time that Garth Brooks saw KISS in concert, he must have come away believing that a man could fly—even a man in ludicrously high-heeled boots and a black-and-silver sequined jumpsuit and cape, his face caked in white mask makeup. KISS helped Brooks form an important part of his performing routine, the part that his insurers must hate (or love, given how much they must charge him for coverage): When Garth took off and flew across the stage during his early 1990s shows, he wowed the audience and must have felt like a member of KISS, albeit one in a cowboy outfit rather than science-fiction space gear. The explosions, swathes of dry ice and "lightning" flashes that became a part of Garth's shows were inspired by KISS (he hasn't yet breathed fire or spat blood like they once did, though, thankfully).

KISS was not the first rock act to employ such explosive stagecraft, and they were not the first American band to take British glam rock and make it sound all-American (thank Alice Cooper for that), but back then they were the hardest-working, longest-touring, and most persistent of the mid-1970s submetal bands to last the decade and beyond. They were also one of the first live acts that the teenage Garth saw perform, along with Queen, for whom Freddie Mercury supplied most of the onstage drama. Mercury eschewed big hair in favor of a big mustache, a leotard, and camp preening—no way would Garth try to emulate Freddie, but Gene, Ace, Paul, and Peter gave him great ideas.

Formed in New York in 1973, the band—bassist and singer Gene Simmons, guitarist and singer Paul Stanley, lead guitarist Ace Frehley, and singing drummer Peter Criss—decided on having a gimmick from the outset because so many bands had succeeded with one. David Bowie had his space alien Ziggy Stardust, Vince Furnier had his nightmarish killer Alice Cooper, the New York Dolls were garish transvestites, and Elton John rocked his piano wearing excessive glam outfits, platform heels, and enormous spectacles. KISS's glittery outfits and white pancake face paint had roots in early sci-fi movies like *Flash Gordon* (compare Emperor Ming and Gene Simmons), kabuki, Pierrot (see Sensational Alex Harvey Band guitarist Zal Cleminson), and British glam rock (see Sweet, the Glitter Band, and Slade). Their music was similarly influenced by contemporary glam and soft rock, but it was always played with an energy and panache that few of their peers could match.

Despite their debut pseudonymous album (1974) failing to sell, their record company boss, a man named Neil Bogart—who'd started his label Casablanca intending to make KISS superstars—invested in two further albums (*Hotter Than Hell*, 1974, and *Dressed to Kill*, 1975). Their lack of success almost bankrupted Casablanca, but KISS had built a reputation as a great live act and building a sizeable live following. Thinking laterally, Bogart ordered a live album to be recorded and released quickly, before he went out of business. KISS's *Alive!*, released in late 1975, was a hit and supplied the band with their first hit single ("Rock and Roll All Nite"). Their next album, produced by Alice Cooper's producer Bob Ezrin and titled *Destroyer* (1976), became the bedrock for their future success.

In 1978, KISS became the first group ever to simultaneously release solo albums by each member of the band. The eponymously titled albums were true solo efforts, with no KISS member appearing on any but their own release, and they sold incredibly well, although not as well as *Alive 2*, their second live album, on which you

can hear a "live" version of the song that Garth Brooks would later record. He didn't know it then, but Garth saw the band when they were coming to the end of their first, legendary phase of success. The original lineup didn't last into the 1980s, and Peter Criss left KISS in 1979.

In 1994, Garth was delighted to be able to contribute a track to *Kiss My Ass: Classic Kiss Regrooved*, a tribute album timed to coincide with the band's 20th anniversary. He chose to record a version of "Hard Luck Woman." It was originally written by Paul Stanley for Rod Stewart, but Rod declined the chance to record it, possibly feeling that it was too close to sounding like "Maggie May." So KISS recorded it for their *Rock and Roll Over* album (1976), and also released it as a single. By the time Garth recorded the song, only Stanley and Simmons remained of the original lineup, but they were there on stage with him as they performed "Hard Luck Woman" live on *The Tonight Show*. The band did

Garth performing "Hard Luck Woman" with KISS (Paul Stanley, right) on *The Tonight Show* with Jay Leno, July 13, 1994.

not wear makeup. Garth appeared in a pristine black cowboy hat, blue shirt, and silver-buckled belt on blue jeans. It is an odd sight, with Stanley and his permed, jet-black hair and black vest in stark contrast to Garth's Sunday smart look, but the sound is great and Stanley's harmonies work well with Garth's hard-edged vocal.

In an interview in 1998, Paul Stanley recalled visiting Garth backstage after he'd seen him perform. During the show, Stanley said he was smiling as Garth swung over the audience's head, got them to sing along with him, and generally entertained everyone in a very active manner. As they met in the dressing room, Garth took his hand and said, "Anything that you saw out there that you liked, you were responsible." He meant it, too.

At the end of 1989, there was a dramatic change at Garth Brooks's
record company, when industry heavyweight Jimmy Bowen took over
Capitol Records' Nashville division. One of his first actions was to fire
all the executives, including Lynn Shults, the man who had signed Garth
Brooks. It could have been a shock to Garth, being a new kid at the label,
but it proved to be the beginning of a mutually rewarding relationship
between the young, soon-to-be-superstar and the veteran record
company man who'd become his new boss.

Everyone in the business who knew him, knew that Bowen—since
he had all round record company skills—liked to be both executive and
producer for his artists. However, after meeting Garth, Bowen recognized
a unique talent, and as he said in an interview at the Country Music Hall
of Fame in April 2014, "Garth has the smartest business head of any artist
I've known." He was aware that Brooks's debut album, as good as it was,
hadn't fully embraced the current digital technology available to top-
flight studios in Nashville, but he also knew that Allen Reynolds, Brooks's

LEFT: The radio microphone allowed Garth to act his songs, not just sing them.

producer of choice, existed somewhat apart from the mainstream for a reason. He did things the way he'd always done them, and the results were pristine and exemplary. Bowen simply wanted Brooks's music, his genre-busting rock and roll meets country sound, to be as state of the art in its production as humanly possible. Garth Brooks, the ultimate team player, was very happy working with Allen Reynolds, and Bowen always listened to what his artists wanted—as Reba McEntire would testify.

Garth found Bowen's marketing mind completely in sync with his own. Bowen trusted Doyle and Lewis to work all their promotional angles and simply added veteran record company marketing man Joe Mansfield to the Brooks cause at Capitol.

Bowen and Brooks were both larger-than-life charismatic characters. They made a great music business team and were able to get across what they wanted from the company with clarity and emphasis. Once Bowen saw Brooks in concert, he completely recognized the enormous sales potential he had in his company. He showed Brooks his trust by not interfering when choosing singles to be released. Bowen knew that what Brooks and Pam Lewis were doing regarding grassroots marketing was working supremely well, and kept out of their way. Importantly, though, he instructed Capitol to spend marketing and promotions budgets on Garth Brooks—and knew that they'd all benefit from doing so.

Sophomore albums are typically tricky for many recording artists. The debut is filled to the brim with songs that have been in gestation for a long time. All those years of writing and/or finding songs are preparation for an album that in essence has taken years of work. The followup, by contrast, usually comes while dealing with a whirlwind of other activity. In Brooks's case that included interviews, radio tours, award shows, and promotional activities. To find new material, set aside time from the schedule to record songs, and have the ability to see the bigger picture for the album is no mean feat. *No Fences*, released in the summer of 1990, was a remarkable follow-up album, though, taking up where the debut left off and further developing the country with a pop sensibility that he and producer Reynolds had forged at Jack's Tracks Studios the year before.

Respected music critic Alanna Nash of *Entertainment Weekly* magazine was immediately impressed. She wrote on September 21, 1990: "On *No Fences*, country's hottest new 'hat act' continues to display a wide streak of individuality. Garth Brooks offers the same mix as any other traditional country performer—ballads, honky-tonk, and the occasional kick-'em-up rhythm tune—but he usually finds off-the-wall ingredients to put in it, such as 'The Thunder Rolls,' a cheating song cast in a Gothic mold. He also has a feel for white-trash anthems, like 'Friends in Low

Places'....Like Elvis, Brooks knows how to make lower class sexy."

Nash picked up on the "hat acts" tag that would be part of Nashville culture in the 1990s. It started with George Strait, of course, and when Clint Black and then Garth enjoyed dramatic success wearing Western headwear, most male country artists followed suit. Of course there was more to Brooks, Black, and Strait than Wrangler jeans and a Stetson, and the three spearheaded a resurgence of popularity in country music. All three understood that everything they achieved hinged on excellent material on their records, not just what was worn on their heads.

Garth Brooks was an above-average songwriter, but he proved to be an excellent song finder. Although he'd discovered "Friends" before he signed with Capitol Records and sang it for his final demo session, it didn't quite fit with the debut. The writers of the sing-along bar anthem, DeWayne Blackwell and Earl "Bud" Lee, had met Brooks when he worked in the boot store and used him to demo the song. They liked him and his version of their song, so they agreed to keep the tune for him. Brooks recorded it for *No Fences*.

Brooks knew "Friends in Low Places" was a hit, but just how big he could never have guessed. A blue-collar underdog song with a rousing chorus, it was perfect Brooks concert fare. It also showed his genius in finding material that had integrity. Brooks wasn't a bar guy; he hardly drank at all. But songwriters Blackwell and Lee lived the honky-tonk life. Indeed, the title came from a lengthy drinking session; when asked how he was going to pay the bill, Lee said casually not to worry, because he had, he said, "friends in low places." It was a heaven-sent country song title, and both Lee and Blackwell knew it. They lived with the song for a while until it came into shape one afternoon in a twenty-minute rush of creative inspiration.

The song had a huge PR lift when Brooks's mother inadvertently gave an Oklahoma radio station an unofficial recording of it. Capitol Records was forced to release "Friends" early because it went down so well with stations and listeners alike. They were justified when the drinking anthem made it to #1 on the *Billboard* chart within eight weeks. The tune later won both the Academy of Country Music and Country Music Association awards for Single of the Year in 1991.

The bootleg leak of "Friends in Low Places" certainly caused an industry stir and helped increase public interest and demand in Garth, but that was nothing compared to the drama that would accompany another single release taken from *No Fences* titled "The Thunder Rolls."

If the powers that be at music video networks CMT and TNN had truly wanted the subject matter of Brooks's powerful musical statement on domestic abuse to slip quietly away, then they could easily have dropped it from their video rotation and refused to give the song much attention or prominence. But instead they issued a ban. And, as anyone

ABOVE: Classic Garth in action, wearing a bespoke rodeo shirt.

with a historical perspective on pop music should already know, bans make artists and songs all the more popular.

In 1957, the Everly Brothers had their song "Wake Up Little Susie" banned by some radio stations because of its supposedly risqué lyrics. It was a move that saw the song leap to #1 on the *Billboard* Pop and Country charts. When the Catholic church banned kids from dancing to Chubby Checker's classic, "The Twist," calling the track "un-Christian," the song went straight to #1 in 1960. In 1977, radio authorities banned the Sex Pistols' "God Save the Queen," thereby bringing much media attention

to the song and sending it to the top of the charts in the UK (although the BBC's national pop radio station refused to play it and pretended that it had only reached #2). Failing to learn from past errors, BBC radio and television banned "Relax," by Frankie Goes to Hollywood in 1983, and watched the song thrive on the attention and shoot to #1.

So, not surprisingly, when country music networks the Nashville Network and Country Music Television banned the music video for "The Thunder Rolls," the song propelled the already-popular Brooks to a wider level of awareness among the U.S. music-buying population. Bob Doyle, Pam Lewis, and Capitol Records could not have created a better crossover strategy for their artist.

"I wasn't particularly pro-video then," Bowen said at his Country Music Hall of Fame Producer Playback interview, "but Garth's "The Thunder Rolls" video moved me. Then we had an incredible stroke of luck when some stations banned it. That's the best thing that can happen, because it gets coverage in newspapers and on TV news." The video was certainly a powerful and dramatic telling of a story that dealt with wife beating and resultant murder. In the film Brooks, in disguise, played a cheating husband who beats his angry wife when he returns home late one night, as a thunderstorm is brewing outside. After he beats his wife, he turns his attention on his daughter, which is when the wife shoots him dead. It was violent, it was edgy, and, most disturbingly, it was also about something very real and something that his audience understood and had to deal with in their own lives.

Before the ban, the Nashville Network asked Brooks to add a voice-over about the violence to the video. The networks' statement said, "If Garth creates a controversial video, he needs to be willing to take responsibility for its social implications." He refused, and co-manager Pam Lewis told the *Tennessean*, "If there's a problem with the video and if TNN feels there's something they want to say about it, that's fine. If they want to run an 800 number or have someone from a woman's group possibly do some sort of video afterword, feel free. But we don't feel it's Garth's place to do it."

CMT had originally put the song in heavy rotation but went along with sister network TNN and dropped it. The channel issued a statement saying, "We are a music channel. We are an entertainment medium. We are not news. We are not social issues. We are not about domestic violence, adultery and murder," as they explained why they had made a "conscious decision with the input of our viewers to pull it."

The ban and its subsequent publicity saw the song hit the top of the chart, but more significantly it gave Brooks national prominence when women's groups thanked him and campaigned to have the ban lifted. Then, when rock-and-pop music channel VH1 added the song to their playlist, Brooks inadvertently broke into the rock-and-roll world.

NO FENCES

(CAPITOL NASHVILLE)

RELEASED

August 20, 1990

RECORDED

Jack's Tracks Recording Studios, Nashville

PRODUCER

Allen Reynolds

CHART POSITIONS

#1 *Billboard* Top Country Albums;
#3 *Billboard* 200

SINGLES

"Friends in Low Places," "Unanswered Prayers,"
"Two of a Kind, Workin' on a Full House,"
"The Thunder Rolls," "Wild Horses"

TRACKS

1. The Thunder Rolls (P. Alger/G. Brooks)
2. New Way to Fly (K. Williams/G. Brooks)
3. Two of a Kind, Workin' on a Full House
   (B. Boyd/W. Haynes/D. Robbins)
4. Victim of the Game (M. D. Sanders/G. Brooks)
5. Friends in Low Places (D. Blackwell/E. Lee)
6. This Ain't Tennessee (J. Shaw/L. Bastian)
7. Wild Horses (B. Shore/D. Wills)
8. Unanswered Prayers
   (P. Alger/L. Bastian/G. Brooks)
9. Mr. Blue (D. Blackwell)
10. Wolves (S. Davis)

Traditional music-business wisdom has it that second album releases are notoriously difficult to get right. With this sophomore release, though, Garth Brooks turned that old cliché on its head and produced one of the most successful country music album releases of all time. It took six weeks from release to get there, but when *No Fences* made #1 on the *Billboard* Country charts, it stayed there for six weeks. More remarkably, though, it made #3 on the *Billboard* 200 LP chart, and stayed in the Top 40 for 126 weeks. Only Shania Twain did better, and then her *Come on Over* (1997) only bested it by a week. On the face of it, the success of this album was hugely surprising. No other country act had come even close to enjoying such enormous crossover appeal, even those who, like Dwight Yoakam, Lyle Lovett, and Steve Earle, had been deliberately marketed to rock and pop audiences. But then, none of them had recorded a song as naturally infectious and catchy as "Friends in Low Places." Owing perhaps something to the two "Rowdy Friends" singles of the 1980s by Hank Williams Jr., the Dewayne Blackwell and Bud Lee song that Garth had demoed for them before recording his debut album had stuck in his mind. It has a perfect mix of ironic cowboy attitude, blue-collar irreverence, and a catchy-as-heck chorus. Garth recorded it at pretty much the same time as Mark Chesnutt, but Team Brooks saw its potential and insisted that it be released as the album's lead single, thus getting it out first. It made the top spot on the country charts in early October. It was only the first hit to be taken from the album, and the last of the four,

Stripes became the signature look.

"The Thunder Rolls" sealed the status of the album as a true classic on release in April 1991. In sleeve notes that accompanied the album's rerelease in 1998 (when "Wolves" by Stephanie Davis was added to the track list), Garth wrote that he still occasionally plays *No Fences* and is still very proud of it, and stands by it. Anybody would.

The video controversy and quality of "The Thunder Rolls" won Garth a whole new audience. When, later that year "The Thunder Rolls" won the CMA Video of the Year award, it was more than justly deserved.

Something else happened in 1991 that played a tremendously significant role in Brooks's success story. It was an industry matter, and one that affected country music in general, but Brooks in particular. May 25, 1991, saw a seismic shift in country music's place in pop music in America when *Billboard* changed the way it measured sales for its charts. It began to use a new system called SoundScan that scanned barcoded sales data in stores across the country. Before the SoundScan development, sales figures were collected by phone-calling sample record stores across America and asking what records they'd sold most of during the previous week. It was hardly accurate, but it was the way the RIAA had always done things.

America had changed since the original chart system had been introduced, of course. Consumers didn't only buy albums from record stores any more. The retail landscape looked very different than it did in the '60s and '70s. This was the Wal-Mart generation, buyers at a Bible belt superstore chain that grew out of the South and spread rapidly across the United States after launching on the West Coast in the beginning of 1990. With barcodes counting for chart analysis, stores like Wal-Mart that had previously not figured in any sales reckoning began to really count. And not surprisingly, given the rural demographic, country music sales were far higher than anyone had believed when Wal-Mart's sales were taken into account. Country music had been ignored and dismissed by the industry until 1991. Now it was very much on the map.

"The numbers don't lie," Jimmy Bowen told the *Los Angeles Times*'s Chuck Philips on December 8, 1991. "Take country music for instance. Garth's domination of the pop charts is changing the status of country in the industry as a whole. All of a sudden, all these pop music record executives see Garth sitting on top of the charts ahead of Prince and Mellencamp for eight weeks straight, and they're saying to themselves, 'Hey, I got to get me a guy like that.'"

The new accounting was in place when Brooks's next album, *Ropin' the Wind,* was released in September 1991. The record had received advance orders for more than 4 million copies and it entered the *Billboard* pop album charts at the top spot. That was a feat never previously achieved by a country music artist.

7

Altered Ego

September 1991 was a pretty momentous month for Team Brooks. After winning the creditable but junior-grade Horizon Award in 1990 (a newcomers' special) most artists, if they are lucky, graduate to Best Male or Female Artist, and some, if they achieve longevity and superstar status, will crown it all with the ultimate CMA award, Entertainer of the Year. But such was Brooks's rise to prominence, his sales volume, and the fact that he outshone everyone in the "entertainment" stakes that his next step was to win the coveted Entertainer of the Year award, bypassing the usual intermediate steps to the top.

But then, very few country acts would be reviewed the way Steve Morse did for *Boston Globe* in August 1991. "Country star Garth Brooks is one wild 'n' crazy guy. His albums are fairly tame affairs, accenting classic country and traditional honky-tonk music. But his concerts are another story. How many country singers stress strobe lights, smoke bombs and rock-concert volume? How many duck walk across stage, playing air guitar? How many climb a rope ladder and hang out over the crowd, wailing Billy Joel's 'You May Be Right, I May Be Crazy'?"

That same year Garth also picked up Country Music Association prizes for his "Friends in Low Places" single, the album *No Fences*, and best video for "The Thunder Rolls." The awards show was held at the Opry House, a few miles outside of Nashville. The ceremony proved to be big news in 1991, not least because President George H. W. Bush and the first lady were in the Opry House. In those more innocent times the local newspaper, the *Nashville Banner*, printed a map of the Bushes' journey to the Opry House from the airport, complete with highlighted vantage spots to get a good view of the couple. A sniper's guide perhaps, but this was friendly, down-home Nashville, and terrorism had not yet become public enemy number one in America.

The good-natured Brooks caused quite a stir when he gave a thank-you speech and appeared to forget that a certain George was in the audience. "This is cool. It's funny how a chubby kid can just be having fun, and they call it entertaining. I know this embarrasses these two guys every time I say this, but I don't think any entertainer is anything without his heroes. I love my Georges—George Strait and George Jones—and I want to thank you guys for being so good to me. . . . No offense, Mr. President. I didn't think about that. Sorry." This brought a visible chuckle from the president and first lady. The president, of course, had the last say in the matter, uttering very prophetic words, "It's easy to see why America loves country music. Country music loves America."

With Brooks's third album *Ropin' the Wind* entering the *Billboard* pop chart at #1 in September 1991 (which was a historic first), many Americans had clearly decided that they liked country music, or at

least Garth Brooks's version of it. Some in country circles were already whispering that Garth Brooks's music wasn't really country at all, but at Capitol Records in Nashville, Jimmy Bowen for one saw his new superstar's success as opening the doors of potential acceptance and affection for all his artists. He regarded Garth's extended reach as offering up to them a new and enthusiastic fan base.

Country music, invented and manufactured in the South, had for too long felt limited by its genre and its image. Perhaps Dwight Yoakam expressed it best, philosophically, when we talked in his office in the Capitol building in Hollywood. He felt, he said, that historically there was a "kind of racism" against hillbillies.

ABOVE: Garth began using
video back projection
for shows in 1992.

Country music was different. It hadn't changed as much as pop. It treated its fans differently and loved to keep its subject matter simple and rural, retaining an essence of innocence.

By doing that, however, the Nashville record business had long realized that it was limited in its sales reach by only catering to its hardcore audience. From the days of Patsy Cline through Chet Atkins and the strings dominated Nashville sound of the '60s, to the likes of John Denver and Eddie Rabbitt in the '70s and '80s, country music artists had tried to cross over into the mainstream. As Chet Atkins told me in his office in 1994, "everyone in Nashville, whatever they tell you, has had a hankering to sell more records. To sell more records you need to sell country music to pop fans. It's as simple as that. Dolly did it. Kenny

Rogers did it. Garth Brooks did it. But did country music cross over, or did those special artists cross over?"

Ropin' the Wind included seven of the album's ten songs written or co-written by Brooks, which was a remarkable achievement given the inhuman workload he'd been under for the past twelve frantic months. It proved to be the record that pushed Brooks into Dolly/Glen Campbell/ Kenny Rogers territory. Its popularity with non-country music fans was proof that the material and production—arguably his and Allen Reynolds's greatest moment—was justified in their attempt to fuse country, folk, pop, and rock and roll into one both joyous and sensitive sound. The underdog theme to the lyrics is still there with the steadfast opener, "Against the Grain," while the rodeo and cowboy songs are especially poignant, especially the album's first single, the touching Larry Bastian–penned "Rodeo." This wanderlust lament had begun life with a different title, though, as Brooks explained to Tom Rivers for the 1995, Westwood One, "Garth Brooks Story" radio special: "I went all over this town trying to get it cut. The song was called 'Miss Rodeo,' and it was written for a woman to sing, and no one would sing it. I crawled on my knees to Trisha Yearwood, I said please you got to hear this song. And she goes, 'Garth I'm sure it's perfect, I don't understand the song because I'm not from that part of the country.'"

"The River" reaches for the philosophical grace of "The Dance," although the images are a bit too grandiose. The brooding number was written with Victoria Shaw, a young writer who had moved to Nashville to become an artist. She told me in an interview with the American Music Channel in 2010, "Initially I wanted to be a performer and came to Nashville to seek a record deal—like so many other people do. Then I discovered the Bluebird Café, found the songwriter community, and I had the ability to write hit songs. And the great thing has always been that songwriting gives you the ability to make your own hours, and of course once I had kids, going on the road was not a good option. So I have been very blessed." Brooks's managers Lewis and Doyle introduced Shaw and Garth at a Country Radio Seminar prior to the release of his debut album. The two were friends first, writing partners second. During a lengthy dry spell in the middle of a writing session at Shaw's house in Nashville, the two young writers took a break and popped on the new James Taylor album. Suddenly, Brooks jumped up and stopped the record in its tracks. Shaw recalled the moment in an interview for the Nashville Songwriters Association International's *Story Behind the Song* series: "He literally picked up a guitar and just went, 'You know a dream is like a river...' He had probably the first few lines. They just came out, and it was like, 'Oh, OK, that's where we're going.' Although, I did try to talk him out of (using the word) 'vessel.' I thought that was a weird word, and now 'vessel' is one of my favorite words..."

Brooks tried the song out for the *No Fences* album but apologized to Shaw when he and Reynolds failed to make it work in the way he wanted. But the dramatic song simply would not go away, and Brooks gave it another shot during the sessions for *Ropin' the Wind*. That time around studio magic happened. The ballad became one of Garth's stage show highlights through the 1990s. Victoria Shaw, during her NSAI interview, fondly remembered the irony on the moment that they listened to their rough recording of "The River": "He's sitting on the floor and I'm sitting on the couch, listening to it over and over, and he said, 'Can't you just imagine a stadium full of people waving their lighters, singing this song?' And I thought, 'Oh my God, he's so delusional. People don't do that in country [music].'"

Once again Brooks had displayed an uncanny ability to put himself in the minds of his audience. It was that trust in his fans that allowed him to really step outside his country music comfort zone and record Billy Joel's "Shameless." This wasn't a country song, which helped to explain how all of a sudden pop stations were playing a Garth Brooks record. The folks at Capitol were so enthused by the song that they planned on hiring independent pop radio promoters to push the song to pop stations and finally break Brooks as a genuine, bona fide pop star. But Brooks understood the nature of the record business in the United States better than some at his label and, along with Doyle and Lewis, resisted their attempts to do so. It was a decision rooted in the territorial nature of the radio business in the United States. If Team Brooks actively went after pop stations, some in the country radio community would feel that he was deserting them for more lucrative, greener pastures. And since Brooks was very much a part of the Nashville community in the early 1990s, and

"Don't change a thing. That's one of the best gimmicks a band can have."

GARTH BROOKS

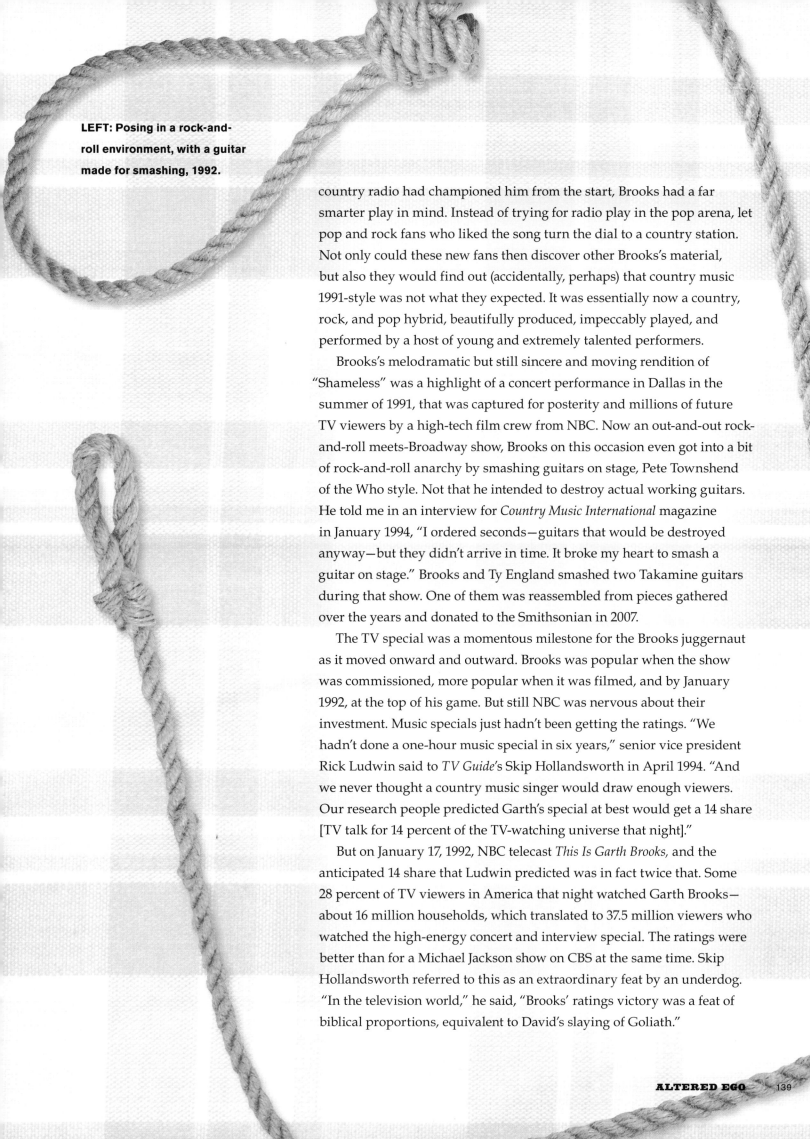

LEFT: Posing in a rock-and-roll environment, with a guitar made for smashing, 1992.

country radio had championed him from the start, Brooks had a far smarter play in mind. Instead of trying for radio play in the pop arena, let pop and rock fans who liked the song turn the dial to a country station. Not only could these new fans then discover other Brooks's material, but also they would find out (accidentally, perhaps) that country music 1991-style was not what they expected. It was essentially now a country, rock, and pop hybrid, beautifully produced, impeccably played, and performed by a host of young and extremely talented performers.

Brooks's melodramatic but still sincere and moving rendition of "Shameless" was a highlight of a concert performance in Dallas in the summer of 1991, that was captured for posterity and millions of future TV viewers by a high-tech film crew from NBC. Now an out-and-out rock-and-roll meets-Broadway show, Brooks on this occasion even got into a bit of rock-and-roll anarchy by smashing guitars on stage, Pete Townshend of the Who style. Not that he intended to destroy actual working guitars. He told me in an interview for *Country Music International* magazine in January 1994, "I ordered seconds—guitars that would be destroyed anyway—but they didn't arrive in time. It broke my heart to smash a guitar on stage." Brooks and Ty England smashed two Takamine guitars during that show. One of them was reassembled from pieces gathered over the years and donated to the Smithsonian in 2007.

The TV special was a momentous milestone for the Brooks juggernaut as it moved onward and outward. Brooks was popular when the show was commissioned, more popular when it was filmed, and by January 1992, at the top of his game. But still NBC was nervous about their investment. Music specials just hadn't been getting the ratings. "We hadn't done a one-hour music special in six years," senior vice president Rick Ludwin said to *TV Guide*'s Skip Hollandsworth in April 1994. "And we never thought a country music singer would draw enough viewers. Our research people predicted Garth's special at best would get a 14 share [TV talk for 14 percent of the TV-watching universe that night]."

But on January 17, 1992, NBC telecast *This Is Garth Brooks,* and the anticipated 14 share that Ludwin predicted was in fact twice that. Some 28 percent of TV viewers in America that night watched Garth Brooks—about 16 million households, which translated to 37.5 million viewers who watched the high-energy concert and interview special. The ratings were better than for a Michael Jackson show on CBS at the same time. Skip Hollandsworth referred to this as an extraordinary feat by an underdog. "In the television world," he said, "Brooks' ratings victory was a feat of biblical proportions, equivalent to David's slaying of Goliath."

ROPIN' THE WIND

(LIBERTY)

RELEASED

September 2, 1991

RECORDED

Jack's Tracks Recording Studios,
Nashville

PRODUCER

Allen Reynolds

CHART POSITIONS

#1 *Billboard* Top Country Albums;

#1 *Billboard* 200

SINGLES

"Rodeo," "Shameless," "What She's Doing Now,"
"Papa Loved Mama," "The River"

TRACKS

1. Against the Grain
   (B. Bouton/L. Cordle/C. Jackson)

2. Rodeo (L. Bastian)

3. What She's Doing Now (P. Alger/
   G. Brooks)

4. Burning Bridges (S. C. Brown/G. Brooks)

5. Papa Loved Mama
   (K. Williams/G. Brooks)

6. Shameless (B. Joel)

7. Cold Shoulder (K. Blazy/K. Williams/
   G. Brooks)

8. We Bury the Hatchet (R. W. Kimes/
   G. Brooks)

9. In Lonesome Dove
   (C. Limbaugh/G. Brooks)

10. The River (V. Shaw/G. Brooks)

The third album is distinctly different from the previous two in appearance, if not sound. Using the same producer, working with pretty much the same team of musicians, and in the same studio, the album was never likely to be a huge departure from *No Fences*. Yet the packaging of this album is very different. Brooks established something of a "look" for himself that was unique in country music. He'd done so with boldly and symmetrically patterned shirts as much because they'd proved to be so useful during live performances—even people way back from the stage could tell which blur of movement up there was Garth because he was the only one in that shirt—as they did for making him stand apart from the other hat acts in the country charts. Alan Jackson had a huge white mustache and long hair peeking out back of his white Stetson; Clint had an enormous black Stetson; George Strait had his belt buckles and white Stetson. Garth needed something apart from the Stetson that he'd worn on the covers of his previous releases, which is where the vibrant blue-and-black striped shirt came in so handy. Turning toward home for his shirts, Garth found "Mo" Betta Clothing, run by a former rodeo champion named Maury Tate out of Apache, Oklahoma. Shirt makers for rodeo riders, the success of the company had been a surprise to Tate, who sold his first shirt to a competitor at a rodeo—it was the one he'd been wearing and sold it on request because he had no money. "Mo" Betta shirts

A romantic rodeo cowboy in Hi-Tops, not Ropers.

have to be hard wearing, comfortable, and unique to each purchaser (or at least the bespoke ones are; now you can purchase off-the-shelf shirts). Garth wasn't falling off steers, but he worked as hard while on stage for over an hour as rodeo riders did during their 8- to 10-second rides in the ring. Serendipitously, the striped shirt proved to be fashionably timely (in 1991 stripes were in on catwalks as well as rodeo rings) and striking enough to make it part of Garth's look. It also said to all those rodeo fans in America that while pop fans had discovered their fave country star, only they recognized the rodeo reference made with the shirt.

This Is Garth Brooks introduced Brooks to millions of new fans, all of them potential record buyers.

Joe Mansfield, vice president of marketing and sales at Brooks's record company, told Chuck Phillips of the *Los Angeles Times* in January 1992, that "Brooks' management and Brooks himself understood the power of TV. We saw the show as a one-hour commercial. We figure about 38 million viewers tuned in to watch Garth. That's 23 million more folks than have purchased his records."

One of Mansfield's key marketing strategies, and one that Brooks agreed with wholeheartedly, was promoting Brooks's catalogue as opposed to just his most recent release. Most record companies let past albums fall by the wayside as soon as a hot new release is available. "It's the industry norm, but I could never understand why they looked at it that way," Brooks told me in 1994. "There are too many albums that get lost and ignored."

Capitol was renamed Liberty after Bowen made something of a power play for more control at his offices in Nashville, as opposed to those in L.A., New York, and London. He'd done so on the back of Brooks's economic strength and power, and subsequently ensured that marketing money was made available to re-promote Brooks's debut album and *No Fences* as well as heavily advertising *Ropin' the Wind*. The third album sold more than 150, 000 copies the week the TV special aired and went back to the top of the albums chart. Significantly, his first two albums also shot up the chart, with *No Fences* at #3 and the debut album, *Garth Brooks*, settling at #10. No other albums in the Top 20 showed any real increase in sales that week. The TV special had broken Brooks into a new market.

Garth Brooks had enjoyed—if that's the right word—a most dramatic and unheralded rise to the top in a ridiculously short period of time. In less than two years he had gone from a nobody, Clint Black–chaser, to a national crossover superstar. The fame, fun, and all that was wondrous at the start was beginning to weigh heavily, though.

Label head Jimmy Bowen expressed his concern to Neil Pond of *Court America* magazine in December 1992. "The pressure on this young man is incredible. Unlike a lot of artists he makes every decision himself, controls every aspect of his career. Plus, he's the centerpiece of this whole country explosion. He's worked hard to do in three years what it usually takes six or seven years to do: become a household name. There's just a tremendous amount of weight on his shoulders." Brooks found his own peculiar and idiosyncratic way to deal with the surreal universe he had found himself in. As the demand for interviews and autographs grew and requests for visits to sick children increased, he developed the third-person strategy to help deal with the phenomenon of Garth Brooks.

He explained his approach to Robert Hilburn of the *Los Angeles Times* on June 26, 1992: "Garth is not difficult to understand if you look at him as two different people. There's GB the artist and Garth the lazy guy just hanging around the house. Here's how the two differ: GB likes the view from the edge; Garth hates heights. GB loves to try new things; Garth is a meat-and-potatoes kind of guy. GB loves the control, responsibilities, and duties that come with the road. Garth enjoys being lazy, dreaming, and other senseless things that people call foolishness."

Those around the Brooks camp had noticed how he had begun to refer to himself in the third person, as if Brooks the superstar was a separate character to the Garth who was discussing him. Childhood friend Mickey Weber noticed the strategy when he went to work for Garth in 1991. He told Hilburn, "When I came out on the road you got to understand that there's Garth Brooks and that's who you're with now…and then there's 'Garth Brooks' who we all work for, including me. When Garth sits and signs autographs for nine hours or whatever at Fan Fair (in Nashville), it's Garth working for 'Garth Brooks.'"

DAN FOGELBERG

In an interview with *American Songwriter* magazine in 1991, Garth Brooks spoke openly about his influences to reporter Al Caudell. Among the list of major singer-songwriters that everyone now knows, such as George Strait, George Jones, Billy Joel, Elton John, and James Taylor, was a name that was perhaps less expected: Dan Fogelberg.

"I think Fogelberg probably influenced me the most," Garth told Caudell. "His songs really made you think that you've got to go with what you feel and follow your heart." Writing on his official website (danfogelberg .com), Bruce Eder compares Fogelberg with James Taylor, citing the latter as the 1960s' definition of singer-songwriter, while Dan was the late 1970s' equivalent.

Born in Illinois in 1951, the youngest of three boys of musical parents, Fogelberg studied art and theater at the University of Illinois in 1969. While there, he performed as a member of a folk-rock band and as a solo performer. While still a student he was spotted performing by Irving Azoff, a rock music manager (he handled REO Speedwagon at the time, among others). After graduation, Azoff sent Fogelberg to Nashville to learn about the art of songwriting, where he not only learned to write songs, but also how to be a session guitarist.

Fogelberg's debut album, *Home Free* (Epic, 1972), wasn't a success, but it was well received by his peers. The follow-up, *Souvenirs* (Epic, 1975), included contributions from some very impressive session players, among them Don Henley, Glen Frey, and Randy Mesiner of the Eagles, who'd been introduced to Fogelberg by Joe Walsh, the producer of *Souvenirs*. Gerry Beckley of America and Joe Walsh played guitar on the record, which also included Graham Nash on

backing vocals and the best-known and regarded steel-guitar player in the business, Al Perkins. Propelled by the single "Part of the Plan," which made #31 on the pop charts, *Souvenir* made #17 on the album chart and established Fogelberg as an AOR artist to watch.

A hastily recorded follow-up release, *Catch Up Angel*, made #23 on the charts in September 1975, and kept Fogelberg on FM radio until he made the crossover to pop radio in 1978, with "The Power of Gold," which made the Top 30 pop singles chart. The following year, with the release of "Longer," Fogelberg became a Top 3 pop star. "It put me on the elevators," he joked about the song, which was prevented from becoming a #1 hit by Queen's "Crazy Little Thing Called Love."

Although "Longer" proved to be his biggest hit single, "Same Old Lang Syne," released in 1980, ran close behind, making #9 on the pop chart. The recording features Randy Brecker playing a superb sax solo riffing on the traditional Scottish tune "Auld Lang Syne." The solo comes at the end of the story-style lyric about two old lovers who meet one Christmas Eve and reminisce while drinking liquor in a car. In Fogelberg's lyric you can see clear inspiration for many of the great Garth numbers that similarly tell stories about lovers who took the wrong turn or made the wrong decision.

"Old Lang Syne" was part of Fogelberg's 1981 album *The Innocent Age*, a double-LP set that was unashamedly based on and inspired by a Thomas Wolfe novel, *Of Time and the River* (1935). Like the book, Fogelberg's album sought to tell the story of the narrator's emergence from youth into manhood, via university and love affairs. That it provided Fogelberg with three further hit singles—"Hard to Say," "Leader of the Band" (about his father, a high-school music teacher

for his whole life), and "Run for the Roses"—is testament to the quality and appeal of the album. The *Greatest Hits* package, released by Epic in 1982, contained all four tracks on the ten-track album.

In 1984, Fogelberg released *Windows and Walls*, and the single from it, "The Language of Love," made #13 on the pop charts, helping to put the LP at #15. The single was a big power-pop anthem for the times and offered no clue whatsoever that the singer-songwriter would take a completely different musical direction with his next release. Using the fine plucking and twanging skills of, among others, Doc Watson, Ricky Skaggs, Chris Hillman, Herb Pederson, and Al Perkins, *High Country Snows* (Full Moon/Epic, 1985) proved to be a very fine bluegrass (or "newgrass," as the trend was mistitled at the time) album. It was his only album to make the country charts, and his last (of 14 in total)

Dan Fogelberg performing in Los Angeles, 1976.

album to make the Top 30 on the pop charts.

Although Fogelberg's sales declined throughout the late '80s and onward, his hardcore fan base persisted and enjoyed a range of different-sounding Fogelberg releases, among them *Exiles* (Full Moon/Epic, 1987), a return to heavily produced guitar-led rock; *River of Souls* (Full Moon/Epic, 1993), an ecologically concerned set of world-rhythmed songs; and *The First Christmas Morning* (Full Moon/Epic 1999), which consists of sixteenth-century songs.

Whatever Fogelberg did, though, right up until his sad death in 2007 (of prostate cancer) was honest. It was the thing that appealed to Garth about Fogelberg (and Taylor). Garth said: "How real they were. When I started writing, that's what I wanted to do."

If Brooks needed something else to keep him grounded, though, he received it in the form of his and Sandy's first child, Taylor Mayne Pearl (named after James Taylor, of course), born on July 8, 1992. He and Sandy would have two more daughters, August (in 1994) and Allie (in 1996). I had seen Garth around kids before, and like a lot of entertainers who never lose their inner child, he was a natural with them. Clearly the responsibility to be a good father and desire to be involved on a day-to-day basis would figure in his thinking for the next installment of his so-far momentous music career. That was a mostly joyous period, but Brooks was exhausted as much as anything, and the thought of devoting himself wholly to his new family seemed very tempting.

Brooks tried to explain that period in his life when we talked in 1994: "I was real tired and really thought about packing it in. I just wanted to pack it in and spend time with my family, but slowly I came to see that I was being too black and white, and that there was a compromise to be made. So, I took time off and paced things a little better."

Jimmy Bowen felt certain that Brooks was far from ready to hang up his hat and boots, but he recognized that this malaise was very real and worthy of his attention. Bowen told Robert Hilburn of the *Los Angeles Times*, "I don't think Garth will retire. He's not the first person to have a baby and deal with the torment of having to go out and work and leave the family at home. He's just got to take some time off to figure it all out, to see how he can balance it all. But the music in him can't stay bottled up. It's got to come out."

While Brooks contemplated a break from his hectic schedule, he would fill the rest of the year with two new albums, a Christmas record, *Beyond the Season*, and a new album proper, titled *The Chase*.

The almost inevitable Brooks backlash—all superstars have one—began in earnest with the release of the first single from the mighty *The Chase* album. Brooks had been in Los Angeles frequently through the summer of 1992, the year of the riots there. Still the dreamer that Victoria Shaw had worked with before his showbiz success, Brooks wanted to

"In Nashville there's people that are ten times more talented than me, ten times better singers and ten times better songwriters."

GARTH BROOKS

express his sincere thoughts about the upheaval he had witnessed, in song. He worked with songwriter Stephanie Davis and poured out some very progressive lyrics, especially for typically conservative country music radio, in "We Shall Be Free." He and Davis wrote about being free to love anyone, that the world's big enough for different views but that in religion, as with all else, everyone has to have tolerance in order to be truly free. They were noble thoughts, but some critics felt he was poking his nose into affairs that musicians shouldn't (especially singing cowboys), and many in country radio found his idealistic liberalism too much to handle. Radio hesitated to play the single, and the song became Brooks first flop (by his lofty standard), making it only to #12 on the *Billboard* country chart. The album was strong, though, and sold almost 500,000 copies in the first week of its release, putting it at the top of both the *Billboard* 200 chart and the country album chart. Critics liked it too, especially those outside the country music Bible belt.

Entertainment Weekly, which had not always been a Brooks champion, said, "*The Chase* is Brooks' most mature and ambitious album. If he can alter country's traditionally redneck attitudes toward blacks, homosexuals, and women, Brooks' feat as a record seller will pale by comparison. The fat boy in a hat is looking like country's savviest reformer ever."

Brooks was proud of his stand for social change, even if it was controversial and lost him some influence in the business. He told me in 1994, "I will always say what I think. I know I've lost support in places because of it, but I've survived this long by being straight and sticking with what I believe in. So I'm not gonna stop now. To make people think about a specific subject, however controversial, is one of the great characteristics of art. That, and trying to bring emotion and understanding to areas that trouble people. I was talking to a guy who accused me of changing into some controversial character. I told him that just wasn't true. I wasn't singing about particular subjects as a publicity move. I hadn't actually changed at all, but five years ago nobody was very interested in what I had to say."

In the sleeve notes for *The Chase*'s reissue Brooks wrote that the recording of the album came at the most trying time of his life, but it was written when he was seeing a very different America than the one in which he'd grown up. Country music had previously been mostly conservative, prone to nostalgia and idealizing an America of the past that had been born of pioneering spirit. Brooks was a very contemporary country storyteller, though, and his picture of the world set to tunes on *The Chase* was not cozy and reassuring. It would not have been surprising if the album had been rejected by traditional country music fans, but the fact that it sold so well was testament to how much Brooks had altered perceptions of the genre that he was revolutionizing.

THE CHASE

(LIBERTY)

RELEASED

September 22, 1992

RECORDED

Jack's Tracks Recording Studios,
Nashville

PRODUCER

Allen Reynolds

CHART POSITIONS

#1 *Billboard* Top Country Albums;
#1 *Billboard* 200

SINGLES

"We Shall Be Free," "Somewhere Other Than the
Night," "Learning to Live Again," "That Summer"

TRACKS

1. We Shall Be Free (S. Davis/G. Brooks)
2. Somewhere Other than the Night (K. Blazy/
   G. Brooks)
3. Mr. Right (G. Brooks)
4. Every Now and Then (B. Mondlock/G. Brooks)
5. Walking After Midnight (A. Block/D. Hecht)
6. Dixie Chicken (L. George/M. Kibbee)
7. Learning to Live Again (D. Schlitz/S. Davis)
8. That Summer (P. Alger/S. Mahl-Brooks/
   G. Brooks)
9. [Something with a Ring to It
   (R. A. Tippin/M. Collie)]
10. Nightrider's Lament (M. Burton)
11. Face to Face (T. Arata)

A year after *No Fences*, which was still a Top 10 album on the country charts, *The Chase* appeared with a black-and-white themed cover and shirt. There may have been something significant in the black-and-white thing, because on "We Shall Be Free," Garth and Stephanie Davis extol the view that life isn't as simple as that, despite the hope that things could be. Elsewhere the familiar Brooks symbols of thunder and storms appear, while songs tell stories about a man trying to get over a lost love ("Learning to Live Again"), a widow trying to find solace in the arms of a younger man who's never felt love before ("That Summer," written with his wife), and the thorny subject of violence against women (Tony Arata's "Face to Face"). Garth considers this to be his "most personal" album, and he wrote that there's more of him in it than their releases. He wrote five of the ten songs on the original release ("Something with a Ring to It" was added to the reissue), and there are two cover versions of well-known numbers, "Walking After Midnight" (a hit for Patsy Cline) and Little Feat's "Dixie Chicken." Both songs had been closely associated with performers who died young—Lowell George, the Little Feat singer and co-writer of "Dixie Chicken" of heart failure at age 34, Cline in a plane crash at 30, the same age as Brooks was when he recorded this. The year that he spent working on this LP was spent touring, expecting his and Sandy's first child, negotiating a new recording deal, and

When things were black and white.

wondering if he could keep going at the pace he'd
established and make it through. And what exactly does
the title refer to? *No Fences* had implied a limitless life
of freedom; *Ropin' the Wind* suggested attempts at
the impossible. *The Chase* is of what, or whom? It sure
isn't fame, fortune, or love and marriage as far as Brooks
is concerned. It suggests a search for something, an
urgent movement in a forward direction.

8

If Tomorrow
Never Comes

Garth Brooks became an entertainment superstar during a decade that would be remembered mostly for giving the world grunge music, Bill Clinton, Starbucks, and the first bleeps of a fully functioning Internet. The United States of America prospered through a remarkable period of peace, economic growth, rapidly declining crime rates, and a budget surplus in the 1990s. The feel-good factor was tangible throughout the country as the economy increased in size by some 4 percent each year from 1992 to 1999. Almost 2 million new jobs were created each year, while unemployment was slashed from an 8 percent high just before Clinton became president, to less than 4 percent in 2000. Home ownership increased from 64.2 percent in 1992, to 67.7 percent at the end of the decade. Average household income went up by 10 percent over the same period, and the national murder rate was almost slashed in half over the decade.

Kids started reading again thanks to the phenomenon of the J. K. Rowling–penned *Harry Potter* novels, while American television entered a golden age of comedy with *Seinfeld*, *Frasier*, and *Friends* leading the way. It was also the period when Americans felt the coolness of dial-up Internet access as the digital revolution began, sparking the beginning of the Apple revolution in technology, design, marketing, and retail.

The optimism and exuberance of the decade was perfectly reflected by the upbeat enthusiasm of a musical act like Garth Brooks—defying easy categorization by crossing musical boundaries that were becoming redundant in a swiftly changing cultural universe. The pyrotechnics, his use of radio microphones, the drama of swinging from ropes, and the sheer theatricality of Garth Brooks shows may have seemed incongruous and consequently distasteful in harsher eras, like the 1970s or post–9/11 America. But in 1992, anything seemed possible, and Brooks was busy proving that to be true.

Just as Jimmy Bowen had predicted, Garth Brooks's success saw an increase in sales for a raft of other country acts who followed in his wake. Billy Ray Cyrus, in the year his daughter Miley was born, burst on the scene with *Some Gave All*, which sold in excess of 5 million copies in 1992—not in the Brooks league, perhaps, but a dramatic increase in numbers for country music all the same. Other artists, from Reba McEntire to Alan Jackson and Travis Tritt, sold a healthy couple of million albums each time they put out a new record in the mid-1990s. It was a bona fide

LEFT: Garth in a "Mo" Betta shirt.

PREVIOUS PAGE: Garth in
more relaxed mode on stage.

country music boom. *Billboard*'s Top 200 album charts began to feature more than five country acts in the Top 20 simultaneously, and, for the first time, they were there on a regular basis.

"This isn't just a repeat of the *Urban Cowboy* craze of the early '80s," Jim Dobbe, vice president of sales merchandise at Wherehouse Entertainment, told the *Los Angeles Times* on September 29, 1992. "What pop audiences are responding to in Garth and Billy Ray are singers who grew up on rock 'n' roll. Country music isn't just a Nashville or Midwest thing anymore. It's big in Manhattan Beach too."

Nobody, not even country music's greatest opponents, could deny that something was happening with this new wave of hillbilly artists. SoundScan proved correct a theory that many in the country music industry had held for a long time. Country music, they claimed, was much more popular than the record business ever gave it credit for. Now Nashville had proof. The new sales-data set editors around the world to check out Nashville and country music for culture features. Throughout the decade the media gave more attention to country music than it had ever done before. New York–, L.A.-, and London-based magazines and newspapers sent writers to report on the Southern phenomenon. Even those looking to burst some Nashville balloons wound up enthralled by the Brooks-led phenomenon.

"There's no formula for me. When I'm hot I can do the lyrics, the melody, everything."

GARTH BROOKS

Nashville's major labels, inspired by Brooks's dramatic success, signed more acts than they had in the 1980s, looking, of course, for their own Garth, or even better, a bigger and more-popular Garth. That didn't happen, but in trying, more acts were given the opportunity to flourish and grow. New labels began to open offices in Music City and immediately found more success than their West and East Coast divisions were enjoying—chief among them Arista Nashville, who scored big with

Alan Jackson, Brooks and Dunn, Pam Tillis, and Diamond Rio.

Country Music Television (CMT) was launched as a younger and hipper country music cable version of its close relative the Nashville Network (TNN). The channel saw rapid growth and, as we saw, played a crucial part in Brooks's rise when it banned the "Thunder Rolls" video. CMT's general manager, Hal Willis, explained to me in 1993 that CMT reflected the fact that country music in the 1990s was filling a void in America's music scene. It was the closest genre around at that time to the classic rock sound of the early 1970s, as pop radio as a whole preferred hard rock or dance music. CMT appealed to those disenfranchised music fans who wanted something in the middle. Not quite easy listening perhaps, but adult oriented with some rock and plenty of great melodies.

Brooks and his cohorts had that by the truckload. "Our research showed that CMT viewers were looking for that Eagles country-rock sound, and Nashville was giving it to them. Content and production values of country music videos improved very quickly in the early 1990s, and the format looked slick, contemporary, and a perfect country music companion to MTV and VH1."

In 1992, buoyed and inspired by country music's sales impact, CMT took the pioneering step of launching the network internationally with CMT Europe and making its programming available in more than fifty countries across the continent. In tandem with the growth of cable and satellite television, CMT picked up strong fan bases in key markets, notably the United Kingdom, Germany, and some former Eastern Bloc countries, among them Poland and Hungary. The move was significant, not just in giving CMT a wider reach but also by building the marketing infrastructure necessary for an artist with vision and ambition to play for an international audience, in the same way that pop and rock artists and bands had always done.

Not that it was all smooth sailing. Garth Brooks is "either the dumbest s.o.b. I've ever seen or the smartest," Liberty Records boss Jimmy Bowen told Jack Hurst of the *Chicago Tribune* in October 1993. At the time, Bowen was referencing Brooks's outspoken and very controversial attack on music retailers who sold used CDs. Noting that artists received no income from the sale of previously owned albums, Brooks felt he was protecting artists, but for an artist earning millions of dollars for himself via sales, the stance was perceived as overreaching and greedy by the unenlightened. At Brooks's prompting, to begin with at least, Liberty kept his 1993 album, *In Pieces*, out of stores that sold both new and used CDs. The retailers, outraged, filed antitrust suits against Liberty though, and parent company Capitol backed down, subsequently shipping the album all over.

Despite Garth's resistance to secondhand retailers, *In Pieces* sold over a million copies in just three weeks. It proved to be a dramatic return to the business after he had taken a six-month break from touring, and naturally led some to question whether the singer's anti–secondhand retailers stance was one staged simply to get publicity for his latest release and upcoming tour. Anyone who thought that can't have known Garth at all though, and it's not as if *In Pieces* needed such publicity.

During a long bus ride to a 1996 country music festival in Poland, Brooks's pal, the country artist Steve Wariner, told me that he felt Brooks was often misunderstood. "This whole marketing major thing grew and grew, and some people came to see everything he did or said as being part of some cynical, grand marketing strategy. I don't believe that it was. Garth just has a gift for attracting attention, maximizing the exposure, and he will always say what he thinks. He always has."

IN PIECES

(LIBERTY)

RELEASED

August 31, 1993

RECORDED

Jack's Tracks Recording
Studios, Nashville

PRODUCER

Allen Reynolds

CHART POSITIONS

#1 *Billboard* Top Country Albums;

#1 *Billboard* 200

SINGLES

"Ain't Going Down ('Til the Sun Comes Up),"
"American Honky-Tonk Bar Association,"
"Standing Outside the Fire," "One Night a Day,"
"Callin' Baton Rouge," "The Red Strokes"

TRACKS

1. Standing Outside the Fire (J.Yates/G. Brooks)
2. The Night I Called the Old Man Out (P. Alger/K. Williams/G. Brooks)
3. American Honky-Tonk Bar Association (B. Kennedy/J. Rushing)
4. One Night a Day (G. Burr/P. Wasner)
5. Kickin' and Screamin' (T. Arata)
6. Ain't Going Down ('Til the Sun Comes Up) (K. Blazy/K. Williams/ G. Brooks)
7. The Red Strokes (J. Garver/L. Sanderson/J. Yates/G. Brooks)
8. Callin' Baton Rouge (D. Linde)
9. The Night Will Only Know (S. Davis/J. Yates/G. Brooks)
10. The Cowboy Song (R. Robinson)

The black-and-white checks of *The Chase* turned red and black for the follow-up album. A third straight #1 country-and-pop debut release, *In Pieces* is packed with hits—five of the singles taken from it between July 1993 ("Ain't Going Down…") and November 1994 ("The Red Strokes") were Top 10 country hits. "The Red Strokes," despite the presence of a crying steel-guitar riff, was the exception. Oddly though, that turned into Garth's biggest hit in the UK (where it made #13 on the national pop chart). Perhaps the influence of Dan Fogelberg on the song helped it in the UK, whereas in the States the influence of Billy Joel on "One Night a Day"—which can hardly be called a country song except for the fact that it's Garth singing—made that single a much bigger hit. The whole of *In Pieces* is—ironically, given the title—a more complete and generic-sounding release than *The Chase* had been. As was becoming the norm, Garth co-wrote five of the songs, and for the opening track (and hit single) "Standing Outside the Fire" he worked with California-based singer-songwriter Jenny Yates. They were introduced by Bob Doyle, who'd signed her to a publishing deal long before he met Garth, and they shared a lot of the same musical influences. She and Stephanie Davis co-wrote "The Night Will Only Know" with Garth, and she also contributed to "The Red Strokes" (along with James Garver and Lisa Sanderson). There's only one cover version on the album, for which Garth returned to his days in Stillwater with Santa Fe,

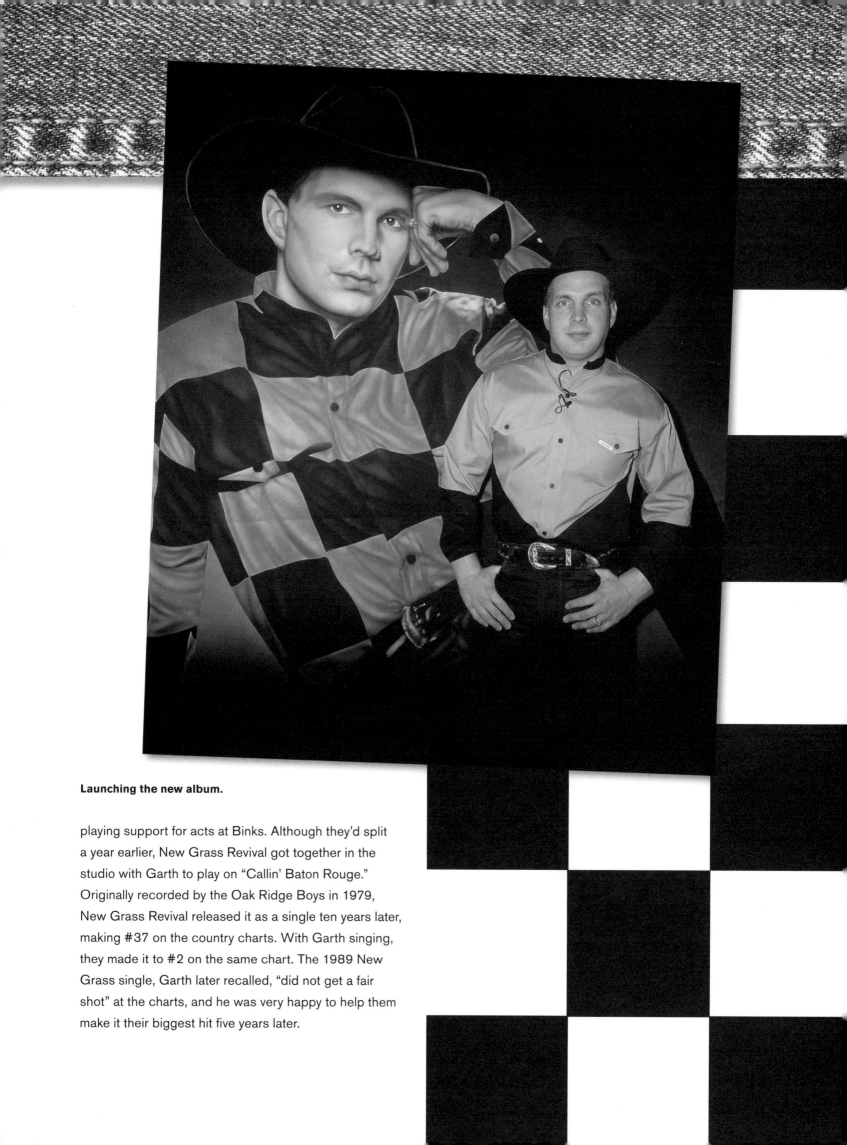

Launching the new album.

playing support for acts at Binks. Although they'd split a year earlier, New Grass Revival got together in the studio with Garth to play on "Callin' Baton Rouge." Originally recorded by the Oak Ridge Boys in 1979, New Grass Revival released it as a single ten years later, making #37 on the country charts. With Garth singing, they made it to #2 on the same chart. The 1989 New Grass single, Garth later recalled, "did not get a fair shot" at the charts, and he was very happy to help them make it their biggest hit five years later.

Garth's live shows were selling out in record numbers. His concerts were more dramatic than ever, with flames shooting across the stage and a rain machine drenching the stage on "The Thunder Rolls." Brooks had perfected his flying-on-high-wire act, despite his proclaimed fear of heights, and the demand for tickets to a Garth Brooks show was becoming record breaking, as he told Hurst for the *Tribune*: "In Sacramento, we saw 62,000 people, in Vegas we saw 51,000. We just put the Fargo Dome on sale, 40,000 seats, and we got two nights out of it—and they're talking about a third night because they got 385,000 calls." Brooks was delighted that his audience had not forgotten him, he continued to Hurst, "…to be given six months off and come back and not be forgotten is the neatest gift people have ever given me. To totally shut down TV and everything for six months and come back like you never left…what a sweet, sweet gift."

In Pieces was a solid follow-up to the magnificence of *The Chase*, but critics were less enthusiastic than they had been with previous

LEFT: Garth after performing
with James Taylor at the
VH1 Honors Awards Show
in Los Angeles, 1994.

albums. *Entertainment Weekly* praised it overall but saw a problem with production. "A true master showman, Brooks sees no artificial divisions between musical genres; to him, country means incorporating any style of American roots music he can lay his mitts on. . . . For all his worthy ambition, though, Brooks is ultimately hampered by the time-honored Nashville studio system, which mandates that the same session men play on the entire album. Those players are perfectly adept at a wind-blown power ballad like "Standing Outside the Fire," but their attempts at rock and late-night blues come off as sterile and homogeneous."

But Brooks had an uncanny ability to both comprehend and predict the minor critical backlash. "When you get as big as that, I think its human nature," he told me during a ride in a London taxicab in 1995. "I saw it coming, and I expected it and I think it was almost a relief. It's kind of like a sports team on a winning streak. The pressure just builds so that when they do lose it's a relief and they can start over again. That absolutely happened with my career."

With the new album flying off the shelves, Brooks opted to follow up the successful *This Is Garth* TV production with another NBC-TV special from the Texas Stadium in Dallas, for broadcast in the spring of 1994.

And then, while back at the top in the United States, he planned on disappearing again for a world tour. "The NBC special is going to be one of my last appearances in this country for a long time," he told *TV Guide*'s Skip Hollandsworth in April 1994. "'For the next 2½ years, I'm not going to tour domestically. I'm not going to release an album. There's going to be nothing. I'll tour sporadically in Asia and Europe during that time, but when I'm home, I'm going to spend time with my wife and my daughter and my new baby. By giving everyone a break from us, I think it will help us out more than touring. People back here will be hearing rumors about us in Europe, about our crowds over there, about the show that we're doing—and when we do return, we're going to have 10 new songs and the whole show laid out. You're just going to have to wait until 1997 to see it."

Before he left the country, though, Garth got to appear on the *Tonight Show* with Jay Leno, singing a KISS song, "Hard Luck Woman," backed by the idols of his youth. When asked to participate on a KISS tribute album, *Kiss My Ass: Classic Kiss Regrooved*, he naturally leapt at the opportunity. *Rolling Stone* magazine was particularly impressed by the Brooks track: "Although Brooks' inclusion is the biggest surprise, his version of "Hard Luck Woman"—backed by the rockers of honor themselves—is one of the most faithful covers. Brooks chose his song well, as the original is a country-tinged bar band number."

Following the July appearance with KISS, Brooks embarked on his international adventures in 1994, with gusto and great intention. In the United Kingdom he played the kind of venues usually reserved for rock stars, like the NEC in Birmingham and London's Wembley Arena. The shows opened with power vocals from new RCA Records star Martina McBride, whom Brooks mentored after seeing her on his tours selling merchandise as the wife of his live soundman, John McBride. Her pure country vocals gave gravitas and country cred to an increasingly pop-flavored show that, at times, seemed more about theatrics than they did old-fashioned musical values. But the theatrics astounded audiences and Brooks won rave reviews for his stage show around the world.

His management refused to listen to record company suggestions that he tone down the cowboy aspect of his persona for the tour. Manager Pam Lewis thought the idea absurd—"That's who he was," she told me—and Brooks duly went overseas in full Wrangler jeans and cowboy hat regalia. It caused some mirth on a couple of mainstream TV shows in Britain, where he was gently mocked, but the treatment only endeared him more to the public. Besides, Brooks loved it. He was the underdog all over again, and his competitive edge returned in full force, making his live shows on that European jaunt some of the most exciting and powerful in his career to date.

He played sold-out shows to adoring fans across Europe, through South America to the Far East, and then New Zealand and Australia. Brooks was beloved everywhere, especially in Ireland, where he built a kinship and unexpected rapport with the Irish community. In Britain, hardly a bastion of country music, *In Pieces*, on the back of his tour, topped the UK country chart and somewhat surprisingly made it to #2 on the UK pop albums chart, too. The two singles from the album, "The Red Strokes" and "Standing Outside the Fire," just missed the pop Top 20.

Brooks spent the first part of 1995 working on a new album, *Fresh Horses*, which he would promote with a continuation of that lengthy world tour, warming up again in the United States and taking in Europe and Australia before heading back to America in 1998. Some fans were worried though, that the touring might have affected Garth's songwriting.

Rumors had been rife before the release of *Fresh Horses* in November 1995 that this was going to be the album that made Brooks a genuine pop star, and that he'd cut ties with his country music and Nashville base. That was proven to be not so, and it was never on the agenda, as he explained to the Fort Worth *Star-Telegram*'s Shirley Jenkins on November 21: "Everyone was expecting this album to be pop. . . . I've said it a hundred times. I'm under their flag, and until they get rid of me, I'm gonna stay here. Because I dig doing this. I don't personally think that any of us as artists have touched within 400 miles of the borders of what country music can do. I think there's more ground to explore in country music than I have left in my lifetime to do. So I don't want to go anywhere else. There're too many cool things in this music to find."

FRESH HORSES

(CAPITOL)

RELEASED

November 21, 1995

RECORDED

Jack's Tracks Recording Studios,
Nashville

PRODUCER

Allen Reynolds

CHART POSITIONS

#1 *Billboard* Top Country Albums;
#2 *Billboard* 200

SINGLES

"She's Every Woman," "The Fever,"
"The Beaches of Cheyenne," "The Change,"
"It's Midnight Cinderella," "That Ol' Wind"

TRACKS

1. The Old Stuff (B. Kennedy/D. Roberts/
   G. Brooks)
2. Cowboys and Angels (K. Blazy/K. Williams/
   G. Brooks)
3. The Fever (S. Tyler/J. Perry/B. Kennedy/
   D. Roberts)
4. That Ol' Wind (L. Reynolds/G. Brooks)
5. Rollin' (H. Allen/L. Reynolds/G. Brooks)
6. The Change (T. Arata/W. Tester)
7. The Beaches of Cheyenne (D. Roberts/
   B. Kennedy/G.Brooks)
8. It's Midnight Cinderella (K. Williams/
   K. Blazy/G. Brooks)
9. She's Every Woman (V. Shaw/
   G. Brooks)
10. Ireland (S. Davis/J. Yates/
    G. Brooks)

This was the album that was supposed to be Garth's move away from country and firmly into pop music. On first examination it might have looked as if that was exactly what the man had done—there's no cowboy hat on the cover, no rodeo shirt, not even a full-on photo of Garth Brooks. Instead, there's just a staring eye and the ominous title that suggests the singer is switching to a new ride, right? Actually, no, not at all, as a listen to the first two tracks confirms. "The Old Stuff" (written by Garth with old buddies Bryan Kennedy and Dan Roberts) tells the story of touring with his "pickers" and all their instruments, back before he was famous. "Cowboys and Angels," as the title suggests, is a lovely pure country ballad, complete with a Randy Travis–style catch in Garth's vocals, a crying pedal steel guitar, and a heart-wrenching fiddle. In fact, fiddles feature more prominently in the mix on this album than they had on previous releases. If the first two tracks haven't satisfied country fans that this is an album that they can listen to, then the Charlie Daniels–style avalanche of "The Fever," which makes Aerosmith sound more American than they ever have, must surely confirm that Garth Brooks was sticking with the formula that had made him a major international star. He co-wrote eight of the ten tracks, too. Clearly Garth hadn't been taking a complete break from making music in the two years since the release of *In Pieces*—there'd been almost nonstop touring, of course—but he hadn't been making pop or rock

A fresh look for the new album.

music. The six singles taken
from the album had a mixed
reception, and there are only
two country #1 hits ("She's
Every Woman," co-written
with Victoria Shaw, and "The
Beaches of Cheyenne," with
Kennedy and Roberts). Still,
the album sold more than
7 million copies worldwide,
which was no mean feat for an album that didn't look
like a typical Garth Brooks release, even if it did sound
like one. The notable video from the set accompanied
Tony Arata and Wayne Tester's "The Change" and
focused on the effect of the Oklahoma City bombing
of April 19, 1995. In the film, Garth stands, wearing
all black, on a black surface, faced on three sides by
enormous screens that show news footage of the events
of that day. That was typical Garth Brooks. As was the
statement he made when he refused the 1995 Favorite
Artist award from the ACM because, he said, he thought
that there were more deserving recipients that year.
That's not a pop star gesture at all.

The album was patchier than previous Brooks masterpieces. It still vibrates with his usual *joie de vivre* and sense of humor, and the first single, "She's Every Woman," was as good as anything he had recorded and made the top spot on the charts. But the follow-up single, "The Fever," an Aerosmith cover version, failed to make the Top 20. It was a shock at the time but offered a clue that perhaps megastardom had left Brooks struggling when it came to putting enough time and care into song selection, something he had previously been more than diligent with. The impressive "Beaches of Cheyenne" single released in December did put Brooks back on top of the charts, but the album kind of felt a little worn and tired compared to *In Pieces*.

Entertainment Weekly again liked the album overall but noticed that the songwriting standards had slipped somewhat: "Brooks' writing is uneven, ranging from a ho-hum autobiographical road paean ('The Old Stuff') to a confusing ghost story ('The Beaches of Cheyenne') to a bordering-on-risqué fairy tale ('It's Midnight Cinderella') that adventurously pushes the envelope of country lyrics. This album is more good fun than great music, but even at its thinnest, Brooks' inventive risk-taking continues to set him apart from his paint-by-numbers competition."

Brooks's problem by early 1996, was the same one that affected all superstar acts dating back to the likes of Sinatra and Crosby. Once a performer reaches a certain level of success, they are mostly in competition with themselves. Brooks would be hard pressed to keep finding material of the quality of "The Dance" and "Friends in Low Places" or "The River": No artist can maintain the level of creativity that typically surfaces on the first two or three releases. Audiences begin to take the act for granted, and with new material played against the classics on the radio, it was difficult for Brooks to get out from under the shadow cast by his early recording successes.

Fresh Horses only sold 3 million albums in the first six months of release. Those were healthy and impressive numbers for anyone else, but not for Garth Brooks. Astute as ever, Brooks was aware of the cycles of fame and figured that the world tour could promote the album internationally and leave American audiences growing fonder of him as his absence grew. He told me in 1994, in an interview for *Country Music International,* "Well, two thirds of all records sold are sold outside the United States. So from a business point of view it makes sense to sell across the world. And that's a consideration. But the real reason is far more simple. You see, I don't feel that you and I are so different. I want people to hear my vision and hear the message in songs like 'The Dance.' And if the people don't get it, then fine, but I feel I have to take the music to them. That is a gift to me from God, and I must pass it on to all humans who have a heart."

That sentiment sounded, to many critics, somewhat grandiose and pretentious, but he was never publicly seen acting in an indulgent or grandiose way. Garth only bought expensive cars as gifts for friends and never for himself and his wife; they lived quietly and as unassumingly as possible when not on tour. It was as if Garth the interviewee was becoming more self-centered and ostentatious, while Garth the husband and father was much more his down-home self. There was a growing tension between the two, it seemed though, and while on tour that tension could be dissipated by the effort and energy expended on stage. When alone, not touring, and trying to come to terms with the demands of a growing family though, things were becoming complicated.

Following the world tour and back at home, Garth put together a new album that was not at all grandiose. The dedication on the CD booklet states simply, "This one is for our moms."

Entertainment Weekly, which was always a pro-Brooks media outlet, intuited from listening to his 1997 album *Sevens* that he was not the

same artist and put some of it down to a shake-up at Capitol Records in Nashville. "Much about it seems tentative, from the stripped-down production on songs that plead for a searing electric guitar to a stylistically wide-ranging program (the Jimmy Buffett–like 'Two Pina Coladas,' the Billy Joel-ish ballad 'I Don't Have to Wonder,' the well-crafted Christmas song 'Belleau Wood') that suggests a lack of focus. There's an unfinished quality about it, with a perceptible dearth of big songs: no bankable Tony Arata hit like 'The Dance,' no self-penned power ballad like 'If Tomorrow Never Comes,' and no rowdy 'Friends in Low Places.' You get the feeling Capitol would have sent him back into the studio if it hadn't been so afraid of him."

It's doubtful that Capitol was afraid of Brooks, but he had certainly amassed considerable power there. There had been a vacuum at the company after the retirement of Jimmy Bowen in 1996. After *Fresh Horses* failed to sell well enough (it was a major release for the company at the time and they had high hopes for its success), Bowen's replacement, Scott Hendricks, was eventually replaced. Involved more and more in the marketing and sales strategies for his releases, Brooks was as familiar as anyone with the tactics employed in country music. He warmed to record executive Pat Quigley's marketing and promotion thinking when they first met, as he explained to GACTV.com in August 2007: "He says, 'You know what's wrong with your business?' I'm thinking, 'No, guy from New York, tell me what's wrong with my business.' He said, 'If I can't go get your record today, I'll go get it tomorrow.' I hated the fact that he was right. What do we do for those people who, at that time, would sleep out in the Wal-Mart [parking lot] to get my album right when it came out?" Quigley was looking for ways to keep an artist like Brooks at the top. If it meant producing limited editions and creating special events, that should be the plan. Brooks was impressed, and it wasn't long before Quigley was in charge of his career.

Brooks had lost his original management company when Pam Lewis split from Doyle/Lewis. The changeover at Capitol had been far-reaching, and the planned simultaneous release of *Sevens* and a Garth Brooks concert in New York's Central Park failed to materialize because of it. The concert was, naturally, bigger and farther reaching that anyone could have predicted. The free show on August 7, 1997, brought hundreds of thousands of music fans to the park. At one point there were close to three quarters of a million people watching the show, which featured Garth in his showman pomp, joined by two special guests, Billy Joel and Don McLean.

When *Sevens* did finally get released, it was a sales monster, moving 3.4 million copies in its first five weeks. When sales slowed after that initial push, Quigley showed his worth by promoting it via the hugely popular *Oprah Winfrey Show* on television. Brooks donated half a million

ABOVE: Live on stage in Central
Park, New York, August 1997–
there was a reported audience
of in excess of 750,000.

dollars to Oprah's charity and promised to donate a percentage of
revenue from sales of the new album, as well. In return, he appeared
on her daytime show every day for a week. Subsequently, the album
roared back up the charts.

Working *Sevens* so hard had the desired effect of putting Garth back
in the news and back on top—from where, in one of his more grandiose
public statements, he announced plans to do his best to bring world
peace to the earth. He had told me in 1996 that it was his dream to use
his international tours to meet with world leaders and talk them into
participating in a peace chain and building peace around the world. It
was Bono territory for sure, but whereas the U2 singer's political work
had built slowly, Brooks's peace initiative seemingly came from nowhere.
After telling me of his plan, he moved on to how the media had been
misrepresenting him and not giving him fair press. They certainly failed
to pick up on his peace initiative or to treat it with any seriousness.

LEFT: Running the outfield
during spring training 1998
for the San Diego Padres.

The press was flummoxed by his next career move, though, when he announced that he had another mission to accomplish: become a professional baseball player. To that end he undertook two days of spring training with the San Diego Padres in April 1998, having first overseen the production of his first box set release, *The Limited Series*, a six-CD set of his previous Capitol albums remastered and with extra tracks added (it became the first ever box set to debut at #1 on the *Billboard* pop-and-country charts). He enjoyed the baseball experience so much that, after getting together the tracks for his first live album release, the two-disc *Double Live* (November 1998), he set about arranging to spend more time with the Padres in the following year.

The six weeks Garth spent with the team in 1999 was only partly to publicize the setting up of his Touch 'Em All Foundation (which quickly became Teammates for Kids). For Garth it was also a serious attempt, at the age of 37, to play some pro ball. As he told WRAL.com, "I'm excited, I'm nervous, I'm scared, and it's going to be neat. Make no mistake about it, I'm out there to play baseball." His salary for six weeks ($200,000) went to the charity, while the Padres, who'd had their best-ever season in 1998–99, enjoyed the glare of extra publicity. After the spring training season though, neither Garth nor the Padres continued their association. Of course, he hadn't enjoyed the best of preparations for spring training, seeing as how between the '98 and '99 seasons he'd announced yet another change of career direction and launched Chris Gaines into the world (see pages 176–177).

Also, avid Garth watchers cannot have failed to notice that *Sevens* had contained a heartfelt ballad about a couple in love with people other than their spouses, sang as a ballad with Trisha Yearwood ("In Another's Eyes"). His and Sandy's marriage had been through many trials, some of which were made very public, and for a time at the end of the decade there were persistent rumors that Garth and Sandy's marriage was coming to a mutually agreed end. Whatever the rumors, there was no disguising the fact that as the 1990s ended, Garth Brooks was a troubled man. Perhaps the baseball was an attempt to ease some of those troubles and get him away from the restrictive confines of Nashville. He certainly didn't give up on the game when the Padres passed on him.

In 2000, Garth tried out for the New York Mets, earning more publicity for his charity and the Mets, but after scoring a 0-17 record during spring training with them, no subsequent contract to play was forthcoming. His baseball career came to its final conclusion after a time spent in training with the Kansas City Royals, again without any Major League action, but Teammates for Kids still benefitted hugely.

Before then, though, there were a lot of matters to straighten out back home in Tennessee.

ALBUM

SEVENS

(CAPITOL/PEARL)

RELEASED

November 25, 1997

RECORDED

Jack's Tracks Recording Studios,
Nashville

PRODUCER

Allen Reynolds

CHART POSITIONS

#1 *Billboard* Top Country Albums;
#1 *Billboard* 200

SINGLES

"Longneck Bottle," "She's Gonna Make It,"
"Two Pina Coladas"

TRACKS

1. Longneck Bottle (R. Carnes/S. Wariner)
2. How You Ever Gonna Know (K. Blazy/G. Brooks)
3. She's Gonna Make It (K. Blazy/K. Williams/G. Brooks)
4. I Don't Have to Wonder (S. Camp/T. Dunn)
5. Two Pina Coladas (S. Camp/B. Hill/S. Manson)
6. Cowboy Cadillac (B. Kennedy/G. Brooks)
7. Fit for a King (J. Rushing/C. Jackson)
8. Do What You Gotta Do (P. Flynn)
9. You Move Me (G. Kennedy/P. Pettis)
10. In Another's Eyes (B. Wood/J. Peppard/ G. Brooks)
11. When There's No One Around (T. O'Brien/D. Scott)
12. A Friend to Me (V. Shaw/G. Brooks)
13. Take the Keys to My Heart (B. Hill/ P. Wolfe/T. Smith)
14. Belleau Wood (J. Henry/G. Brooks)

After announcing, in 1994, that he was going to take a couple of years away from America, Garth toured the world. The release of *Fresh Horses*, following an unusual (for him) two-year gap between albums, was welcomed by fans as much for being a country album as anything else. There were no worries that his seventh album would not be all country, and as if tired of playing that game, *Sevens* came packaged with a cover that bore a svelte, hunky-looking Garth in black cowboy hat, white T-shirt, and black jeans, standing in a stable next to rodeo tackle (the title also plays on the fact that there are seven main events in any major rodeo tournament, usually referred to as "the sevens" by riders). The debut single and opening track of the album, "Longneck Bottle" (written by Steve Warner and Rick Carnes), is a faux–Western Swing number sung from the point of view of a man who can't leave a honky-tonk while there's music playing, even if there's a girl waiting at home for him. The album was released containing 14 tracks, a good four more than usual on Brooks's albums, and perhaps that was as much to make up for his having been away for another two years since the release of *Fresh Horses*. Garth only co-wrote six of the songs, but one of those is the lovelorn ballad "In Another's Eyes" (co-written with Bobby Wood, who co-wrote "Talkin' in Your Sleep," and John Peppard). The song was recorded as a duet with Trisha Yearwood and released as the album's second single (making #2 on the country chart). In

ABOVE: Garth and Trosha duetted on this album.

hindsight, the song offers a little hint about the singers' relationship—Trisha divorced her second husband in 1999, the same year that Garth and Sandy separated. At the time, though, critics only remarked on how well their voices combined. It's easy to forget perhaps that Trisha had sung on Garth's very first album back in 1989, and they'd had plenty of practice in harmonizing in the studio. They'd soon get plenty more.

Great art is often a product of tragedy, and the music of Chris Gaines was wrenched from him over a period during which he endured several tragedies.

A contemporary of Garth Brooks in as much as they fought for the top album spots on the American charts throughout the 1990s, because Gaines never tried his hand at writing country music he was never a challenger for Garth's crown. In fact, country music was one of the few genres that Gaines didn't experiment with.

Maybe it was because he was born in Australia, one of the few nations that can claim to be even younger than America, that Chris Gaines didn't feel the burden of having to carry any kind of cultural load. Raised in Los Angeles, where a sense of self is at best tentative and usually fluid, when Garth moved to Nashville and began making country music, Gaines signed his first record deal as part of a band called Crush. Their eponymous album was a hit in 1986, but then the first tragedy to strike Gaines occurred. His co-writer and best buddy Tommy Levitz ("we were brothers," Gaines would always say) was killed in a small plane crash in 1987, and the band ceased to exist.

After two years of grieving and being dangerously close to becoming addicted to various substances, in 1989, Chris Gaines released his solo debut, *Straight Jacket*, and it went to the top of the charts. That title, like so many of his storytelling songs, is a clue to what Garth likes about Gaines. A pun that goes deeper than the initial smile it raises, *Straight Jacket* suggests a madness about the singer who was always willing to admit that he was addicted to sex, that he had to live life to the full, whatever the consequence. In 1990, a second tragedy hit Gaines when his father died from

cancer. That inspired Chris to write and record a new set of songs that were different musically from his debut. Released as *Fornucopia* in 1991, it was a funkier and harder set of recordings than he'd previously released. It included his remake of a song that his father had loved, Ramsey Sellers's "It Don't Matter to the Sun."

Perhaps the loss of his father—with whom Gaines had endured a difficult relationship ever since rejecting his father's wish to become an athlete and not a musician—merely contributed to worsening his reckless attitude toward life. Whatever the root cause, Gaines's way of living life to the maximum led, in 1992, to a third tragedy in the form of a life-changing accident. Driving his vintage red Corvette much too fast in the Hollywood Hills, Gaines fell asleep and drove off a cliff. He awoke as he left the road, he later recalled, realizing that he'd "stepped over the line."

Thankfully, the crash wasn't fatal, but it did leave him very seriously injured and his face disfigured. After two years of surgery and hospital care, during which he had his face and shoulder rebuilt, Gaines emerged a changed man, but still determined to make music and do it his way.

As if life hadn't brought enough tragedy into his short life, early in 1994 Gaines's home in the Hills was engulfed in flames from a brushfire, despite his trying to beat the flames back from the roof of his home using a puny fire extinguisher. He lost everything. Suddenly, Chris Gaines found himself with a new face that was barely recognizable as his, and without any physical objects that could anchor him to a past life.

Still, he released his third solo album later in 1994. Titled *Apostle*, it demonstrated a more spiritual approach to life, albeit one suffused with sexual yearning that attempted to find a sexual healing. The love of a good woman failed to save him from himself and his addiction to sex though, and even after seeking help for sex addiction, he was unable to say no to willing women who for ever sought him out.

In 1996, Gaines released *Triangle*, an R&B-infused album that owed as much musically to Prince as it did Bruce Springsteen. Sadly, the departure from a firmly rock-oriented sound didn't please his record company, and the album wasn't the hit that he'd come to expect. He thought that they didn't promote it properly, and subsequently withdrew from the recording world.

As the millennium approached Gaines decided to compile a *Greatest Hits* package, to which he added a new song titled "Right Now." On it he rapped about how terrible the world was and how it needed love to heal itself. The album was a hit, making #2 on the album chart with only a VH1 special (*Chris Gaines: Behind the Music*), and an appearance on *Saturday Night Live* for which Garth Brooks introduced him (see page 184).

Then, while at the top of the charts and after announcing that he was working on a new concept album titled *The Lamb,* Chris Gaines disappeared. And he stayed disappeared, too—although, it would surprise no one who knew the man if his disappearance was a smart marketing move. Perhaps, the thinking goes, he disappeared in order to build a curiosity about what he was up to. His fans would only grow fonder of him the longer he's gone, right?

But, at the time of writing, it's been fifteen years since he went away. And despite Garth Brooks's public support for Gaines, and his deeply felt desire to make a biopic of his tragic life, Gaines has so far remained reluctant to come out of hiding.

Garth discusses *The Life of Chris Gaines* at a press conference in 1999. (P.S. Garth *is* Chris Gaines.)

Garth occasionally performs a Gaines song in concert—and then we realize what we're missing. But still we await the resurrection of Chris Gaines…

9

Why Ain't I Running?

To be at the top of any game for a decade is a very rare thing. Even in country music, where once a reputation is made a star can remain in orbit—kept there by the most loyal and supportive of fans—to have every release reach the #1 spot on the charts is unusual, to say the least. Actually, it's more than unusual; it's unique. George Strait came close in the 1980s, but his first two albums in 1981 and '82 didn't make the Top 10—although he had #1 releases in the following eight years.

That's partly why Garth Brooks so admired, and was inspired by, George Strait; because of his consistency and excellence. Now, while Garth made the #1 spot on the country album charts with every release he made between 1990 and 2000, he made far fewer LPs than Strait managed in the same period—but Garth's seven #1's (*No Fences* "only" made #2) sits well against George's five (of ten releases in 1990–2000).

But of course, the truly unique thing about Garth the country star was that five of his album releases in his first decade as a recording artist made the #1 spot on the U.S. pop album charts. George Strait barely entered the *Billboard* Hot 100 before Garth's success on the pop charts, and even after Brooks had pioneered country-as-pop-hit albums, George only managed one pop-chart #1 release (he has a career total of five top-spot albums on the pop charts, 1981–2015).

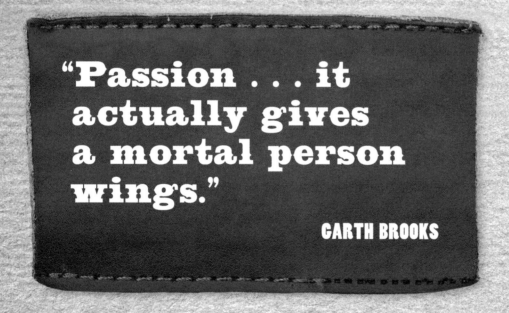

"Passion . . . it actually gives a mortal person wings."

GARTH BROOKS

Garth's first decade in Nashville proved to be momentous in so many ways, of course. He single-handedly revolutionized the country music business, crossed previously unassailable genre boundaries (Johnny Cash managed just three #1 pop-chart hit albums in a fifty-year career, and the last of those came in 2000), altered forever the way that country music live shows could be staged, and generally swept away the conservative,

ABOVE: Although close to
divorce, Garth and Sandy in
2000, were still friends and
companions at awards shows.

PREVIOUS PAGE: Garth's
connection with his audience
makes everyone feel as if he's
singing directly to them.

isolationist policy that Nashville had adopted since the invention of
the Nashville Sound in the late 1950s. By 1999, then, Garth Brooks was
arguably the most powerful man in country music. Of course with great
power comes greater responsibility, and the weight of that responsibility
for the future well-being of country music can only have sat heavily on
Garth's broad shoulders.

The final year of the century was not exactly the kindest that Garth
had lived through, either. After years of struggling to keep their marriage
together, if only for the sake of the children, in the spring of 1999 Garth
and Sandy decided that it was time for them to separate. They didn't tell
anyone except family at first, and it was of primary importance that the
world in general didn't know about the split because the Brooks family
was trying to deal with the very sad and upsetting fact of Colleen Brooks
suffering from throat cancer. She had been diagnosed with the condition
in 1998, and Garth dedicated the single version of "It's Your Song," a live

cut taken from the *Double Live* set, in November 1998, to her. The song was written by Pam Wolfe, a former backing singer for Conway Twitty, who also co-wrote "Take the Keys to My Heart" with Benita Hill, a former backing singer for the Allman Brothers who'd suffered and recovered from non-Hodgkins lymphoma (she co-wrote "Two Pina Coladas" with Garth). Speaking on the release of the single, Garth had said, "I've been looking for the right song to sing for my mother ever since I started making music; the sentiment expressed in "It's Your Song" was what I'd wanted to say to my mother all this time and just never found the words."

One of the awful consequences of her illness was the Colleen was effectively robbed of her speaking—and singing—voice, that same voice Garth had grown up listening to singing him lullabies, country songs,

LEFT: Colleen and Raymond
Brooks on their way to witness
their son being honored at an
awards show in the mid-1990s.

and hymns; she lost the voice that had so comforted Garth and his siblings in the months leading up to the point when, on August 6, 1999, Colleen lost her life. The Brooks family was gathered together at her bedside in the Integris Canadian Valley Regional Hospital in Yukon when she passed away at age 70, after undergoing months of medical treatment.

In a particularly poignant coda to the death of his mother, in 2005, Garth donated $500,000 to the hospital with the aim of their building a women's center and naming it after Colleen. However, when four years later no women's center bearing her name had been built, Garth sued the hospital for missuse of his funds. Giving evidence in court, the Associated Press reported on January 18, 2015, Garth had told how the hospital's president had first suggested naming an intensive care unit after Colleen, before suggesting the women's center idea. That was the one that appealed to him, Garth said, because, "It's my mom. My mom was pregnant as a teenager. She had a rough start. She wanted to help every kid out there." The court found in Garth's favor and ordered the hospital to repay the $500,000 plus another $500,000 in damages. Garth's response, as reported by the *L.A. Times* on January 26, 2015, was to claim that "One day Mom's name is going to go on the women's center right there where the hospital is, but that hospital won't be owned by Integris when it happens, I can tell you that. That's my dream."

Back in mid-1999, when Garth was watching the dreadful end to his mother's life in Yukon and arranging to separate from Sandy in Nashville with as little fuss and pain as possible, he was also concerned with a separation of a different kind. His last album (*Sevens*) had been released in 1997, but Garth hadn't been musically idle in the intervening period. Quite the contrary, in fact.

However, he hadn't been into Jack's Tracks with Allen Reynolds and his usual crew of Nashville pickers. Instead he'd been at the Capitol studios in Los Angeles, with rock producer Don Was, working on a completely different style of music than country. In the process Garth was creating a completely separate identity for himself.

Aware, perhaps, that he had stretched his traditional audience's patience and willingness to listen to music from him that wasn't purely Nashville-based, Garth decided that he would "become" a fictional character to record rock, pop, and soul songs that bore no trace of the usual Garth Brooks musical signatures. Garth's musical taste hadn't stagnated as his success as a country artist grew. He still listened to other types of music, including the soul and funk sounds of Prince as well as the contemporary releases by his old favorites like Dan Fogelberg, James Taylor, and the Rolling Stones—with whom producer Was had recently worked. Their musical inspirations would not sit well within the musical framework that Garth Brooks, country superstar, had constructed, though. So, thinking laterally, Garth created an alter ego who could record songs in different musical styles and adopted a name and persona that country fans wouldn't necessarily be attracted to, but that AOR fans could listen to without prejudice. Garth was well aware of the prejudices that his name evoked among certain music fans, and thought that by releasing the songs on Chris Gaines's *Greatest Hits* (November 1999) he might get a fair hearing from them.

Except that wasn't the whole plan. If the Chris Gaines project had simply consisted of the album release, it might have been received with more understanding by the press. But Garth launched it as being the soundtrack to a movie that was waiting to be made, in which he—who had made some neat music videos but never actually acted in anything seriously—would star. The idea might have been for the project to have reminded people of Barbra Streisand's producing, directing, and starring in the Academy Award-winning *A Star Is Born* (1976), in which she "became" Esther Howard. But Garth was not Streisand, and the idea was so bizarre to the world's press that they were left scratching their heads and wondering if Garth's ego had outgrown his cowboy hat.

A month after his mother's death, Garth appeared in an NBC-TV special looking a little wild-eyed, with graying hair, dressed in all black, and performing with a band in front of a live audience and a huge video screen, onto which photographs of "Chris Gaines" appeared, as Garth described the project. Two months later (November 13, 1999) on *Saturday Night Live*, Garth introduced the show and the guests—one of whom was Chris Gaines. Made up as Gaines, Garth performed the Prince-like "Way of the Girl," and no one on the show remarked on the physical similarities between Garth and Chris, who was presented as being a returning legendary rock star. The album's CD booklet contained a well-constructed story of Gaines's life and career. A very funny and believable VH1 *Behind the Music* "documentary" about Gaines, which included contributions from, among others, Billy Joel, Don Was, and a host of actors, was made, but the movie project never materialized.

The album made #2 on the *Billboard* Hot 200 album chart and sold in excess of 2 million copies, which doesn't exactly make it a flop. It just didn't sell as many copies as a "Garth Brooks" album would have. As the year and the century came to a close, Garth's life was changing, and as he announced to TNN's Crook and Chase in December, it would change drastically in the forthcoming year. "I never, ever thought in my life I'd say this," he told the interviewers, "but music is not the first thing in my life any more." He was thinking about his three daughters, he said. "Those girls somehow come along and they just take your energy and all of a sudden all you want to do is you want to do things that make them smile." His work had kept him away from them pretty much constantly since they'd been born, and pretty soon, he said, "definitely I've got to

RIGHT: Garth with songwriter and producer Babyface (left) and producer Don Was (right) launching *Garth Brooks In...The Life of Chris Gaines*, in 1999.

step up and take care of my responsibility." So, he revealed, he'd "probably lay low" for nine or ten months, plan a big party, and "probably announce our retirement at the end of next year."

There was a big party, held for him in October 2000 by Capitol Records, who hired Nashville's Gaylord Exhibition Center to celebrate his having sold 100 million albums. At the press conference before the event Garth sat down and stated simply, "I'm here to announce my retirement." It wasn't a shock, and he had talked about retiring a few times in the past—the first being in 1992 when Sandy was pregnant. But this time, he continued, according to ABC News (October 27, 2000), "I've done my career with the old saying, 'Burn bright, burn fast.' I wasn't going to be somebody that we could come to really appreciate, like Billy Joel and

James Taylor, and know that their stuff was timeless." He went on to talk
about his and Sandy's intention to divorce (although that wasn't a done
deal yet) and once again put his children at the forefront of his decision
making. "My children and I are together every day," Brooks said. "And
every night I tuck those children in, and I'm responsible for their safety. I
feel good about that. I have asked my wife to be father and mother long
enough. It's time for me to accept my responsibilities, and accept the true
rewards that come with being a father."

In an interview in 2015, with *People* magazine, Garth also told a story
about how he'd heard one of his daughters pronounce a word in an accent
like that of her nanny, and "realized someone else was raising her."

Before fully retiring from making, playing, and promoting music,
Garth owed Capitol an album's worth of material, and plans were
in place for it to be released in November 2001. But at the time of his
retirement announcement only they knew that. In January 2000, the
music industry newspaper *Billboard*'s Chet Flippo asked various country

music executives how they saw a future for their business without Garth in it. Capitol Nashville President David Quigley said, "We've been talking about this for a year. Short term this means we won't have the funding we need to do a lot of the marketing projects that we do, because Garth generated enough money to pay not only for his marketing but also for a lot of other people's marketing, too." So Garth kind of had that on his conscience—new acts might not get the exposure, or even deal, they would if he was still supporting them by releasing records. Quigley continued to lay out his master plan to Flippo: "But the good news strategically for us is that two years ago I stopped just throwing a bunch of new artists out there. So this wouldn't hurt us as much it might a traditional label. Because we're only gonna put one or two new acts out a year anyway. Remember, we've got Garth's catalog."

RCA label group chairman Joe Galante wasn't too bothered, he said, because "In terms of the marketplace right now, over the last year or two, his influence on the sales side has been lessened. So, it's a loss, but I think we'll be able to weather the storm." Over at Mercury Records, Luke Lewis called Garth's retirement "a shame." But, he continued, "We're about to have the biggest country album ever [with Shania Twain] and he set the bar pretty darn high. Being the sort of competitive person that I am, I hate to see him get out of the game."

> ## "My hardest thing was to let go and be happy for everybody, and just to enjoy."
>
> **GARTH BROOKS**

Actually, Garth didn't exactly say that he was getting out of the game completely. As he told Crook and Chase, "I'd like to write songs for other people and write scripts for movies. Writing seems to be what my bag is." After the October 2000, announcement and the public acknowledgment of his and Sandy's separation (they filed for divorce in November 2000; it was finalized within a year), Garth had nothing to do except complete what became *Scarecrow* and get to know his daughters properly.

RELEASED
November 13, 2001

RECORDED
Jack's Tracks Recording Studios;
The Sound Station, Nashville

PRODUCER
Allen Reynolds

CHART POSITIONS
#1 Billboard Top Country Albums;
#1 Billboard 200

SINGLES
"Wrapped up in You," "Squeeze Me In" (with Trisha Yearwood), "Thicker Than Blood," "Why Ain't I Running?"

TRACKS

1. Why Ain't I Running? (K. Blazy/T. Arata/G. Brooks)
2. Beer Run (B Double E Are You In?) (K. Williams/ A. Williams/K. Anderson/G. Ducas/K. Blazy)
3. Wrapped up in You (W. Kirkpatrick)
4. The Storm (K. Blazy/K. Williams/G. Brooks)
5. Thicker Than Blood (J. Yates/G. Brooks)
6. Big Money (S. Camp/R. Hardison/ W. Varble)
7. Squeeze Me In (D. McClinton/G. Nicholson)
8. Mr. Midnight (J. R. Cobb/B. Buie/ T. Douglas)
9. Pushing up Daisies (J. Hadley/ K. Welch/G. Scruggs)
10. Rodeo or Mexico (B. Kennedy/ P. Kennerley/G. Brooks)
11. Don't Cross the River (D. Peek)
12. When You Come Back to Me Again (J. Yates/G. Brooks)

ALBUM

SCARECROW

(CAPITOL/NASHVILLE)

It was launched as being the "final" Garth Brooks album and came a year after he'd officially retired from music. The title may have been a reflection of how he felt emotionally. The final track on the album, "When You Come Back to Me Again," was originally written for a science fiction movie released in 2000, titled *Frequency*, and starring Dennis Quaid. The song was nominated for a Golden Globe. Garth said that he'd written it for his mother, Colleen, and it eulogizes her as a lighthouse shining for him, the lost ship. The album also contains a duet with Trisha Yearwood, "Squeeze Me In," that has the pair sounding as if they're having great fun with the honky-tonking piano and rocking guitars. Likewise the duet with George Jones, "Beer Run," of which Brooks said, "It was the least I've ever been pissed off at getting out-sung. It was an honor to get my ass kicked that day." They performed it live together at the 35th annual Country Music Association Awards show in 2001, at the Grand Ole Opry, and the mutual respect was clearly evident. *Scarecrow* is something of a traditional-sounding country album and bears no signs or sounds of the Chris Gaines experiment that preceded it. Made using his usual crew of musicians, it sounds as much of a whole as any Garth Brooks release. There's a hint of Steve Earle and Dwight Yoakam to be heard in "Rodeo or Mexico," but for the most part the musical influences are classic country, and the songs would not sound out of place on any Nashville-made record of the

July 4th, 2001 at Philadephia Museum of Art.

previous fifty years. It was promoted via three NBC-TV specials aired in November 2001, each shot in distinctly different venues, the most striking of which was the gun deck of the USS *Enterprise*. The shows and the album garnered favorable reviews. The *Daily Oklahoman* critic exclaimed, "Just when you thought country music was set to be taken over by young punks, here comes Garth Brooks to show you how real country sounds." Unfortunately for the reviewer of course, this was not the first of a string of "real country" releases from Garth, but rather a period before an ellipsis. It would be over a decade before there was a wholly new Garth Brooks country album released.

Another Nashville separation and divorce had occurred almost simultaneously with Garth and Sandy's, but at the time it received nowhere near the same amount of publicity, nor did it seem to have anything to do with the Brookses' split. Trisha Yearwood was a friend to the Brookses and had recorded with Garth from the beginning of his

LEFT: In harmony with Trisha
Yearwood, someone he "always
enjoyed being around."

career. Her split from her second husband since 1994, Robert Reynolds (bassist with the Mavericks), was announced in 1999, and divorce quickly followed. It seemed like another case of two musicians whose careers took them in different directions and made it hard to build a home together. Her "starter" marriage, begun when she was 23, to a musician and studio engineer named Chris Latham, had lasted four years (1987–1991). That was when Trisha worked as a receptionist at MTM Records (owned by TV comedy actress Mary Tyler Moore) and sang backing vocals when possible—which is how she met Garth. Speaking to Ellen DeGeneres on November 29, 2013, Garth said about the first time the pair had met, in 1988, "Alright. Here's the strange thing. I can't believe I'm really going to do this. Kent Blazy introduced me to Ms. Yearwood and he goes, 'I knew you were going to like her.' When she left, he goes, 'what did you think?' I said, 'well it's strange, because I felt that feeling like when you just meet your wife, but I've been married for 13 months.'"

The pair had clearly felt a connection, and they worked together on and off throughout the decade. In 2001, as Garth went on to explain to Ellen, he felt that "this was somebody I always enjoyed being around, and we had a lot more in common than I ever dreamed we did. And so we started seeing each other after the divorce and we came off tour. . . . And I've got to tell you if you like her and don't know her you'll love her. If you love her and don't know her you'll worship her. She's the real deal."

In June 2001 Trisha released *Inside Out*, which went to #1 in the country charts and #29 on the pop chart. The first single taken from it, "I Would Have Loved You Anyway," made #4 on the country singles chart. In November of the same year Garth's *Scarecrow* made #1 on both the country and pop charts, and included two notable duets. The first, with George Jones, "Beer Run," is a great, Jones-like rollicking hoe-down. The second is a similarly upbeat number with left-hand rolling piano and rocking riffs. "Squeeze Me In" (a Delbert McClinton and Gary Nicholson composition) is sung from the viewpoint of a man trying to persuade a woman to go on a date, but in Garth's version his duet partner, Trisha Yearwood, sings the second verse, making it sound as if both parties have been trying to persuade the other to get together.

The CD booklet includes a black-and-white photograph of the pair, with Garth leaning over Trisha's shoulder. They look perfectly comfortable together. No one seemed to notice that, following Trisha's success with *Inside Out*, she disappeared from the music business at the same time that Garth did. Both stepped away from the limelight, kept off all red carpets, and didn't enter a recording studio or radio station for four years. Capitol kept releasing singles from *Scarecrow* (four in total), with "Why Ain't I Running?" being the last, in 2003.

It took a disaster and the death of a good friend and idol to get Garth and Trisha in public, making music again. In 2000, Chris LeDoux had been told that he needed a liver transplant or he'd die. Garth had volunteered as a donor and undergone a biopsy, only to find that he wasn't a match for LeDoux. Happily a donor was found, though, and LeDoux had a transplant in October 2000 that was successful. He made two albums in November 2004, before he was diagnosed as suffering from cholangiocarcinoma, a cancer of the bile duct that was terminal. He died on March 9, 2005, in Wyoming. While grieving, Garth wrote "Good Ride Cowboy," and released it as a single in October 2005.

Garth made a surprise appearance to perform the song live at the 39th Annual CMA Awards on November 15, 2005, in Times Square. Later that evening, LeDoux was honored with the CMA Chairman's Award of Merit, which Garth accepted on behalf of LeDoux and his family. LeDoux would probably have been embarrassed by the fuss made about him, as he's fondly remembered for saying, "What I want to be known for, on top of everything else, is that I was a good husband and family man."

In September 2005, Garth and Trisha had broken their retirement in order to perform a duet of Creedence Clearwater Revival's "Who'll Stop the Rain" live, for a TV broadcast titled *Shelter from the Storm: A Concert for the Gulf Coast*. It was put on to raise funds for victims of Hurricane Katrina and raised some $30 million.

Also in 2005, Garth launched his own record label, Pearl, and through it released a four-CD box set and separate single album for sale only through Wal-Mart and Sam's Club stores. Titled *The Limited Series*, the box set packaged his last three albums (*Sevens, Live Double, Scarecrow*) with a new release titled *The Lost Sessions*, which was also made available as a separate CD in an extended format, plus three singles, "Good Ride Cowboy," "Love Will Always Win," and "That Girl Is a Cowboy." *The Lost Sessions* comprised previously unreleased tracks recorded between 1995 and 2000—there were 11 on the CD that came with the box set, and 17 on the individually released edition.

Because *Lost Sessions* and *The Limited Series* were sold in only two retail chains, and not via other stores in which SoundScan was in operation, neither registered for chart placing. It was, on the surface, a baffling decision on the part of Garth and his business managers. However, he and they knew where Garth Brooks fans shopped and wanted to reward them with something that was just especially for them. What did he care for the approval (or money) of the world in general, when he could communicate directly with the people who'd made him a success in the first place, seemed to be the thinking. Perhaps the unexpected release was also something of a wedding gift to fans of Garth and Trisha—he'd proposed to her in the most unexpected and public manner in May 2005. Present at Buck Owens's Crystal Palace in Bakersfield for the unveiling of a Garth statue, Brooks dropped to one knee, removed his cowboy hat, and asked Trisha, "Will you marry me?" She didn't seem to be expecting

ABOVE: Jay Leno chats with Garth and Trisha after they'd performed "In Another's Eyes" on the *Tonight Show*.

it, but said "Yes," and they were married at their home in Owasso, Oklahoma, a little over six months later, on December 10, 2005.

Between the proposal and ceremony Trisha recorded a new album, and *Jasper County* was released in September 2005, making it to #1 on the country chart and #4 on the pop chart. The following year the album was rereleased with an extra track, a duet with Garth that was also released as a single, titled "Love Will Always Win."

Little by little it seemed that Garth and Trisha were working their way back into the music business. Soon enough there'd be a full-time return from retirement announcement to be made.

10
Man Against Machine

When, in 2005, Garth and Trisha had ventured out of their self-imposed retirement to sing a couple of songs in public, fans of both must have been hoping for further ventures into live performance for the pair. However, for a couple of years Garth (and Trisha) retreated to their home in Oklahoma and hunkered down again, raising his daughters in full cooperation with Sandy. However, it soon became apparent that Garth and Trisha were not ignoring the music business, they were actually taking stock, figuring out how best to work with what was a rapidly changing industry. By 2006 it had become clear that the old ways of creating and selling music product were becoming obsolete. The rise and success of Amazon had been surprising and astounding. In 2007, it added music downloads to its offerings for customers, creating its own MP3 player online. For a while before that, Main Street record stores had been in decline, their numbers falling in line with the sales of CDs, cassettes, and vinyl records (many old-style country music stores stocked secondhand records and tapes).

When Amazon announced that they were going to take on Apple in selling MP3s online and offer them in conjunction with CDs on their website, it was giving people the opportunity to choose whether to download just one song rather than buy a whole album. For once though, Amazon was slow to get to market with their MP3s however, and in 2008, Apple's iTunes store outstripped Wal-Mart in music sales for the first time. Ever since the turn of the millennium the country music business had been functioning under the assumption that downloads were for kids, while their fan base, being more mature, would continue to buy physical forms of music—CDs particularly.

At the time Garth announced his retirement in 2000, sales of recorded music were at the highest they'd been since 1973, with close to a billion units of CDs, records, and tapes being sold in America. In 2007, that figure had almost halved, with around 600 million units being sold, LPs having disappeared from the numbers, cassettes close to extinction, and digital downloads on the increase.

In August 2007, Garth announced the release of a double-CD compilation that would be packaged with a DVD containing his videos. He also announced a gig—more, if needed—at a newly completed venue in Kansas City, called the Sprint Center. In what would become the norm for all musical acts, Garth booked the date because he had a forthcoming release and realised that diminished financial returns on CD and download sales needed to be supplemented. Selling live performance tickets seemed like the way to do it. As ever, Garth wasn't wrong.

The compilation, titled *The Ultimate Hits*, was released on his own label, Pearl, and included thirty greatest hits plus four all-new songs. In September 2007, the first single taken from it, a new number titled "More Than a Memory," went straight to #1 on the country charts and seemed a

ABOVE: Garth in action at L.A.'s Staples Center for the fire intervention relief effort, January 2008.

PREVIOUS PAGE: The Garth Brooks World Tour with Trisha Yearwood, at the Pepsi Center, Denver, March 2015.

not too thinly disguised hint that Garth wasn't happy to be just a memory. The live date, initially set for November 5 only—the day before the official release date of the album—was increased to a total of nine, and spanned November 5 to 12, and 14. Garth was only the second performer to appear at the Sprint Center, following the opening gig by Elton John in October. Garth's first date was added to as ticket demand grew within an hour of going on sale. He sold around 140,000 tickets in two hours, and for those unlucky not to gain access to any of the shows, the last of the nine gigs was broadcast live to movie theaters across the country.

By all accounts, the performances were a huge success and Garth appeared to be having the best fun. It was not a surprise then when he announced more live performances, for January 2008, at the Staples Center in Los Angeles. What was a surprise was the price of a ticket:

They were all held at $40 for every seat, and the five performances over only two days sold out within an hour. That the proceeds of sales went to firefighters in the state who'd tackled an unprecedented series of fires around L.A. in the previous year was an added bonus for purchasers.

Trisha was also busy with her musical career at the same time, and in November 2007, she released a new album for a new label. *Heaven, Heartache, and the Power of Love* came out via Big Machine records, which had been established only in 2005, by country singer Toby Keith and former Dreamworks executive Scott Borchetta. Their first album release had been for a young female singer named Taylor Swift. Big Machine was a young and forward-thinking company, and Borchetta—whose father had been a record promoter in L.A. before moving to Nashville at the end of the 1970s—was helping to change the country music business like no one else.

Heaven, Heartache, and the Power of Love received rave reviews and made #10 on the country album charts (and #30 on the pop). It had to

LEFT: With his neighbor, the
biggest country act to have
emerged during Garth's
retirement, Taylor Swift.

compete with a greatest-hits compilation released by her old label (MCA) in September, which made #2 and #22 on the country and pop charts, but both releases put her back at the forefront of the country music scene. So, had the Brooks-Yearwood partnership agreed to return to making and performing music full time in 2008? It seemed not. There were no announcements regarding the career of either following the L.A. firefighters benefit concert. They were still "retired," so what next?

Garth and Trisha were not like other, older country stars, after all. Back in the 1980s, country music stars didn't retire; instead, they moved to Branson, Missouri. Nestled in a bend of the White River where it joins Lake Taneycomo in the Ozark Mountains, the tiny town of Branson came to be a second home for the old country artists who no longer fit in among the New Country artists that first attracted Garth to Tennessee.

In 1987, Boxcar Willie opened a theater in Branson just so he'd always have somewhere to perform, and where his dwindling fan base could assemble and watch him sing. Three years later, he was followed by, among others, Mel Tillis, Jim Stafford, Mickey Gilley, Moe Bandy, and Ray Stevens, who all had their own theaters, named for them, lining 76 Country Boulevard in Branson. Regular performers at other theaters in the town, particularly Lowe's, included Conway Twitty, Loretta Lynn, Waylon Jennings, and Vern Gosdin. By the middle of the 1990s, Glen Campbell and the Osmonds were Branson Theater owners, as was the first major non-country artist to open a place there, Andy Williams (he named it the Moon River Theater).

In 2009, the largest privately owned airport in the United States was built on land owned by Tennessee Ernie Ford in Branson. It cost $155 million to complete and involved cutting the tops off various Ozark Mountains to make the place viable. In 1990, there were fewer than 4,000 residents of Branson; by 2013 that was estimated to have risen to over 11,000, and the majority of the new inhabitants were there to service the country music fans who visited in the tens of thousands every year. What would the population have to be if there was a Garth Brooks Theater in town, wondered many in Branson.

But then, Garth Brooks wasn't actually an "old" country star (he was still in his 40s), and his fan base probably wouldn't want to fly over the Ozarks and wander Highway 76 to visit the Hollywood Wax Museum or the Titanic Museum. If he was going to play any kind of residency at a purpose-built theater, it would have to be somewhere bigger, brasher, more pop than country. In January 2009, Garth performed "American Pie," "Shout," and "We Shall Be Free" with the Inaugural Celebration Chorus at We Are One: The Obama Inaugural Celebration at the Lincoln Memorial. That was a very un-Branson kind of thing to do.

In October 2009, the *Las Vegas Sun* newspaper reported that "Garth Brooks, the best-selling solo musician in history, said on Thursday he was coming out of retirement and was expected to announce an extended concert run at the Wynn Las Vegas casino and hotel." As the Associated Press reported it, the approach to play in Vegas came from Garth to Steve Wynn, via an email that the hotel and casino boss printed, framed, and put on his wall. Garth had asked Wynn if he could perform at the small Encore Theater at Wynn Las Vegas in a solo acoustic performance. When the star-studded audience reacted with wild applause, Wynn set about persuading the singer to book a residency.

"I told him he couldn't afford me," the AP reported Brooks saying. "I was wrong. Wow."

Apparently Garth agreed to the residency as much for Wynn's promise of the use of his personal jet plane, allowing him to play Friday, Saturday, and Sunday but be home for Monday morning. "Every argument we ever had about why we shouldn't do this, he had an answer to," Brooks said. CMT reported the announcement as Garth officially coming out of retirement; however, the singer was adamant that it didn't signal anything except the residency in Vegas, and that there would still be no more touring for him until his youngest daughter reached college. Garth stated at the Vegas press conference that there'd be no touring or recording: "The only place you'll see me is here." Steve Wynn then said that all tickets would cost $125.

The first-night reviews for Garth's performance were good. *USA Today* called the show the "antithesis of Vegas glitz and of the country singer's arena and stadium extravaganzas." The first show was on his wedding anniversary, and Trisha was the only other performer on stage with Garth that night (or any other). He sang songs from his back catalogue and those of the artists that he'd grown up admiring, from Billy Joel and Simon and Garfunkel to Dan Fogelberg and Don McLean. Demand for tickets proved such that the residency lasted for three years, ending in December 2012.

In April 2013, Garth and George Strait performed a duet live at the 48th Academy of Country Music Awards show. On July 6, he joined Toby Keith and a bunch of other country music stars (including Trisha, of course) in performing a sold-out concert at the Gaylord Family Oklahoma Memorial Stadium in aid of victims of that year's tornado disaster (dubbed the Oklahoma Twister Relief Concert). Barely three weeks later, Garth Brooks became a grandfather when his second daughter, August, (who was 19) gave birth to a girl that she named Karalynn. Becoming a grandfather is the kind of thing to make a man take a long look at himself, and a man like Garth may well have thought that, when he really looked at himself, he wasn't done with his career.

In November 2013, Garth's Pearl label released a massive six-CD, 77-song, and 33-video box set titled *Blame It All on My Roots: Five Decades of Influences.* Released only through Wal-Mart and Sam's Club stores (as the

ABOVE: Performing with George Strait at the 48th Academy of Country Music Awards Show, Las Vegas.

FOLLOWING PAGE: The Twister Relief Concert at Garth's old alma mater, the University of Oklahoma.

Limited Sessions had been), it proved to be enormously successful, selling nearly 900,000 copies in its first year of release. Four CDs of the set were new recordings of old songs that Garth had grown up loving, with each dedicated to a different musical style. They were *Blue-Eyed Soul* (including Motown hits), *Classic Rock* (by the likes of Skynyrd and Queen), *The Melting Pot* (largely singer-songwriter numbers), and *Classic Country* (which began with "Great Balls of Fire"). The box made the #1 spot on the *Billboard* Top 200 albums chart, top country albums, and top independent album charts, too. As Christmas 2013 approached, while promoting the set on the *Tonight Show*, Garth looked sincere and eager when he announced that he would be back from retirement permanently the following year, and touring with a band.

It took the best part of the first half of 2014 for Garth to get
everything lined up for his first world tour in thirteen years. In July,
he announced that he'd signed a recording deal with Sony Music
Nashville and that a new album would be out before the end of the
year. He also announced that he'd be playing two dates at Dublin,
Ireland's Croke Park sports ground. They sold out so fast that another
date was added, and then another and another still—he would play
on July 25, 26, 27, 28, and 29. A total of 400,000 tickets were sold—in a
country with a population of 4.7 million. However, due to complaints
from residents of the area in which the venue was sited, the gigs
were cancelled. (Unintentionally, One Direction was the cause of the
cancellation: Their three consecutive nights of gigs in May constituted
the maximum number of evening-held non-sporting events that the
venue was allowed to hold in one year.)

A couple of weeks later tickets went on sale for the first U.S. (and by default the first of the tour) date, at the Allstate Arena in Rosemont, Illinois. Initially there was just one night announced, but as ticket sales began and sold out rapidly, three more were immediately announced. Demand for tickets kept growing, and Garth called a major Illinois-based radio station to promise that he'd keep adding performances until demand was satisfied. He eventually played eleven shows at the venue between September 4 and 14. Ever the pioneer in country music, rather than announcing his tour dates in full and well in advance of the complete tour, Garth added venues and performances at each one at a time. Each venue's box office and website were besieged by Garth fans as soon as they were informed of dates. At the time of writing, the Garth Brooks World Tour with Trisha Yearwood (to give it its full title) was on course to set all kinds of live performance records, from ticket sales to revenue generated and the speed of sell-outs at pretty much every place the tour played—and by June 2015, the venues reached hadn't included Los Angeles or New York. Neither had any dates been announced outside of the United States, and this was to be a world tour—Irish fans continued to wait and plead for rearranged shows well into 2015.

Also in September 2014, Garth announced the launch of his back catalogue in digital format for the first time, but not through iTunes or Amazon, rather, in keeping with his pioneering ways, via a new digital music store named GhostTunes. Its point of difference from Apple and Amazon's MP3 stores is that GhostTunes allows the artists and labels to put a price on their releases and not have to bow to the retailer's demands. As well as his past albums, Brooks's latest album of the first new material he'd recorded in a dozen years, was also announced for release via GhostTunes and garthbrooks.com. Despite limiting the release, *Man Against Machine* entered the country album chart at #1 on release and made #4 on the *Billboard* Top 20 (although Garth told CMT that he wouldn't follow its chart progress). In March 2015 *Man Against Machine* was certified platinum, having sold over 600,000 units.

From early September 2014, until early June 2015, Garth Brooks and Ms. Yearwood (as he refers to her in public) performed over 100 concerts, sometimes playing two in one day. Reviews of shows from fans have unilaterally been very good to great. Garth Brooks has most definitely made a powerful and successful comeback. Part two of an extraordinary career has begun, and it promises to be as exciting and challenging as anything he's done in his pre-retirement career.

Although, given his and Trisha's work rate, they're going to need a long holiday when the world tour does finally end.

MAN AGAINST MACHINE

(PEARL/RCA NASHVILLE)

RELEASED

November 11, 2014

RECORDED

Allentown Recording Studios,
Nashville

PRODUCER

Mark Miller

CHART POSITIONS

#1 *Billboard* Top Country Albums;
#4 *Billboard* 200

SINGLES

"People Loving People," "Mom"

TRACKS

1. Man Against Machine (L. Bastian/J. Yates/ G. Brooks)
2. She's Tired of Boys (A. Williams/G. Brooks)
3. Cold Like That (S. L. Olsen/M. Price/C. Wallin)
4. All-American Kid (C. Campbell/B. Long/ T. McBride)
5. Mom (D. Sampson/ W. Varble)
6. Wrong About You (A. Wright)
7. Rodeo and Juliet (B. Kennedy/G. Brooks)
8. Midnight Train (M. Pierce/M. A. Rossi
9. Cowboys Forever (W. Varble/J. Martin/ D. Dillon)
10. People Loving People (L. T. Miller/ C. Wallin/busbee)
11. Send 'Em on Down the Road (M. Beeson/A. Shamblin)
12. Fish (C. Wallin/W. Varble)
13. You Wreck Me (S. Bentley/ K. Kadish/D. Muckala)
14. Tacoma (C. Smith/B. DiPiero)

Thirteen years after his last album, Garth Brooks unleashed a new one with a title that owed something to science fiction and a cover that made him look like Vin Diesel as a cowboy. The opening, title track sets the tone for all that follows, and it is not "country." It gives a warning in the first person of the threat that man's dependence on machines is proving to be. Launching the album, Garth said in his press conference that "Music has always been a reflection of where mankind is at the time. For 14 years, I have watched heart and soul, dreams and individualism, fighting for their very existence in a world of increasing technology. This album is a reminder to all those who dream, work, and fight for what they believe; do not give up your vision." As if to protect his "vision," Garth's eyes (for the first time in his career) are not visible on the LP cover; instead they're covered by shiny opaque sunglasses. The cover poses Garth as a muscular, unfathomable "man" of the title who will fight against machines on behalf of us all. The cover of the single that preceded the album, "People Loving People," suggested prayer as a weapon against machines, showing the back of Garth's cowboy hat, his hands raised together as if in prayer and in front of a massive congregation (the shot was taken at the Twister Relief Concert in 2013). It didn't sound very country music—like, and "Man Against Machine" is positively all-out rock and roll, with no steel guitar, fiddle, or banjo to be heard. Since Garth had been in "retirement,"

The man to fight the machines.

the country music scene
had, of course, evolved in
the direction that he'd first
taken it. In 2014, Nashville's
biggest star was also the
pop world's biggest star,
just as Garth had been 20
years earlier. Taylor Swift's
October 2014 album *1989*
sold more in its first week
than any album released in
the previous 12 years. Titled
for the year of her birth,
1989 was recorded using
synthesizers, samplers,
and more producers than
musicians. *Man Against
Machine* uses Nashville
musicians, many of them
old friends, and just one
producer. Both artists,
though, are on the same
side in the battle about
how to sell their music,
which was not through Apple or Spotify. Machines,
watch out…

AUTHOR'S DEDICATION

To my wife Eva, the bravest person I know

PICTURE CREDITS